POST-COLONIAL HOKUM

Revisiting the recent history of Britain and the Commonwealth

By
Graham Tottle

Copyright © Graham Tottle 2016
This book is sold subject to the condition that it shall not, by way of trade or otherwise, be lent, resold, hired out, or otherwise circulated without the publisher's prior consent in any form of binding or cover other than that in which it is published and without a similar condition including this condition being imposed on the subsequent publisher.
The moral right of Graham Tottle has been asserted.
ISBN-13: 978-1522972310
ISBN-10: 1522972315

DEDICATION

I'm massively indebted to my family and friends in many countries. It would be invidious to try to name individuals. So here are just a few key people:

Mr. Mohamed Nor, sometime Head of RISDA (The Rubber Industry Smallholders' Development Authority, Malaysia, Dr. Colin Leakey, Fellow of Kings College, Cambridge, Major Tom Ellis, MBE, Head of Extension Services, Western Province, Uganda, Owekitinisa Paulo Bukeribuga, Mutwale Bufumbira, Nick Feeland, MA, FBCS of Masdar worldwide development consultancy, Alison Tottle, photographer, Upali Aranwela, Planning and Development Manager, JEDB, Sri Lanka, Professor Gordon Black DIC, Professor of Computation, Manchester University, Ashok Hegde, Programme Manager, International Computers (ICL), Dr. Judy Rose, Botanist, ARC (Agricultural Research Council) East Malling, Dr. Dujaily, sometime Director of Planning in Saddam's Government, Dr. Fred Robson, Head of Management Studies, Royal Agricultural College, John Ratcliffe, Year 11 student at Tytherington High School.

CONTENTS

Introduction 3
Chapter 1 An Agricultural Revolution 14
Chapter 2 Beginnings 18
Chapter 3 A New Recruit 23
Chapter 4 First Endeavours – Constitutional Development 29
Chapter 5 Industrial Development 48
Chapter 6 Religion, Health, and Medicine 64
Chapter 7 Historical Background to the Uganda Protectorate 68
Chapter 8 Entomology – the Study of Insects 73
Chapter 9 Agricultural Research 84
Chapter 10 Agricultural Extension 92
Chapter 11 National Finance and Exploitation 101
Chapter 12 The Scrombles – Whatifs – The Previous Government Syndromes – The Devonshire Course 106
Chapter 13 Agricultural Management 115
Chapter 14 Environment and Wildlife 125
Chapter 15 Culture, Language, and Sport 130
Chapter 16 Law and the Commonwealth 133
Chapter 17 Commonwealth Failures: Iraq and Sudan 136
Chapter 18 Transport 161
Chapter 19 Mining 172
Chapter 20 Conclusion 175
About the Author 190
Index 192

ACKNOWLEDGMENTS

Warm acknowledgements to:
Rhodes House Library
British Museum
The Guardian
BAE Systems
Uganda Tourist Board
Metalique
Century of Flight.

Introduction

I was a District Officer (government official roughly equivalent to a British medieval sheriff) in the South West of Uganda for five inspiring years just before independence in 1963. Followed by twenty years programming and managing big mainframe software in ICL (International Computers Limited) in Manchester, then twenty years as a consultant in computing for development. This involved working for the UN Food and Agriculture Organisation and World Bank and EU and DFID in 21 Third World countries, most from the Commonwealth. As the saying goes, "Been there, done that." Unlike most of the pundits who fashionably attack the Empire.

Like Marc Antony in Julius Caesar, I "speak what I do know". But Shakespeare's Marc Antony was pulling the wool over the four citizens' eyes, whereas I am not.

This gave me an affection for and understanding of these 21 countries which is way beyond the hypercritical hokum spoken by many journalists and even many historians of today.

Talk to a typical ex-District Officer like me and he's likely to say, with a rueful but reminiscent and friendly smile: "But, you know, it just wasn't like that. Not at all."

So what was it like?

I hope to select from my own experience in many countries some of the key fallacies written, e-mailed, or spoken by prominent writers, politicians, and journalists like Ryszard Kapuscinski, Tony Benn, Jeremy Paxman, Michael Palin, Simon Schama, Maria Misra, Seumas Milne, Ernst Gombrich or Neil, sometimes in direct correspondence. Let us group them together as "hokumites" Their fallacies have corrupted our view of the British Empire and the Commonwealth, and with it our view of our own destinies as Brits (in my case an Anglo-Scot) and members of the Commonwealth. Do we really want to deride and break up our heritage and our influence on the world? An influence sometimes bad, far more frequently good.

I hope also to select correspondence and views from people who have taken a much more positive view of the Empire and Commonwealth, like Melvyn Bragg, Andrew Marr, John Sergeant, Nial Ferguson, Paul Kennedy, or Chris Patten. For what it's worth, my view is that in Uganda, for example, the British Protectorate brought happiness and civilisation to peoples who, before, had suffered indescribably under their rulers as we'll see. A thousand years' worth of progress was achieved in Uganda in a short 62 years of clock-on-the-wall time. It's a view which many Ugandans have shared.

Was this colonial oppression? Or are the critics preaching post-colonial hokum?

A popular Monty Python sketch demanded:

"What did the Romans ever do for us?"

"Er... how about roads?"

"Yes, roads of course, ok... But what else?

"Er... how about laws?"

"Yes, laws of course, ok... But anything else?"

And then followed a reluctant list; baths, aqueducts, forums, cities, water wheels, etc. Here I hope to do similarly for the Empire and Commonwealth as I've known it.

I'm starting with a look at four modern communicators to give an overview of the issues, and then covering this field in more depth from my own experience, as against the critics, over fifty years.

Kapuscinski

Our first protagonist is Ryszard Kapuscinski:[1]

He is a widely respected and quoted writer, delightfully readable, though his background was as a journalist from Poland, in the Second World, i.e. Communist Europe. One would have thought that his anti-British, anti-Western background would have been taken into account by teachers and academics since the seventies. But not so. His message was a message they wanted to hear, a message which was fashionable, and perhaps a message which would further their careers and reputations. Only very recently has a biography in Polish by a great admirer, now disenchanted, revealed the truth about him.

Graphic from the Guardian.

---

[1] *Riszard Kapuscinski – A Life*, by Artur Domoslawski, was published in translation from the Polish in 2012. An absorbing review by Ian Birrell as published in the *Observer* on 18th August 2012.

In *Shadow of the Sun*, page 35, he wrote about the colonial officials:

"A **minor clerk** from Manchester received on arrival in Tanzania a villa with a garden and swimming pool, cars, servants, holidays in Europe etc. Members of the colonial bureaucracy lived **truly magnificently... beyond all measure and reason**." (Kapuscinski goes on to ascribe to this all manner of post-colonial evils.)

Let's try to map this onto reality, first horizontally for my contemporaries, and secondly vertically, for the district in which I served:

Horizontally:

"**Minor clerks**" – Our generation of administrators were in fact all graduates with good arts degrees, mostly from Oxbridge, all with a postgraduate year on the Devonshire Course at Oxford, all fairly fluent in two Ugandan languages (mandatory, pass at intermediate level or you're fired) and trained in an impressive range of highly relevant subjects: law, social anthropology (tribal cultures), agriculture, ecology, history, economics, administration... We earned slightly less than our contemporaries in the home civil service, and were able to save nothing.

We had **one heavy car, a splendid Standard Vanguard, vital for our jobs**, and no electricity, mains drainage, TV, radio, cinema, etc. Poor food, 250 miles from a major hospital, and so on. I never saw a swimming pool in a private house in the entire country! As for the "holidays" in Europe, our leave, once every three years followed the same patterns as did and do commercial firms today (I'm not grumbling – it was an immensely satisfying life). Kapuscinski must have known all this. And yet he pursued his "truly magnificent" myth at length. Just what, in the days of political correctness, his readers hoped to hear.

Vertically:

Take a similar vertical view for Kigezi District, where I worked for senior government officers:

15 professionals from seven different Commonwealth countries (note "Commonwealth" – English 5, Indian 1, Scottish 2, Canadian 2, Ugandan 2, New Zealander 2, Zimbabwean 1), all but one graduates in their specialty, mostly long-service professionals in agriculture, veterinary services, medicine, education, law, forestry, survey, entomology, mines, civil engineering, police. Their careers after leaving Uganda were usually distinguished.

So, much of imperialism, especially late imperialism, was a major achievement, and there's no harm in saying so as long as it's done without arrogance and with friendship. These historic links can, just as in the francophone world, be a bridge between the peoples involved.

*

Our next protagonist is TV presenter **Neil Oliver** – his absorbing TV programme on the missionary who dedicated his life to areas in Central Africa, David Livingstone (The Last Explorers, Jan 2012) ends with a savage denunciation of the Europeans' carve-up of Africa in 1882 – popularly denigrated as "The scramble for Africa". It was indeed a carve-up, but to whose benefit, why, and are there any credible "Whatif" studies (to quote current computer fashions) which explore the alternatives? What would have happened if the Africans had been left to themselves? What would the balance of happiness have been? I explore this later in the book, after the nature of life in Africa in pre-colonial times has been described.

*

Our next journalist is **John Sergeant**. He is a deeply respected BBC reporter and a very prominent personality on national TV. A railway enthusiast, he produced and presented a fascinating study of Indian railways, their history and the central and essential part which they played and still play in the economy and culture of the entire subcontinent. His interviews frequently involved working railway people, who reflected with affection and pleasure on their railways and on the part of the Brits had played in creating this wonderful network. Without it India would not function, and, against the West's profligate waste of fossil fuels on air travel, it's environmentally very kindly.

Sergeant reached a glorious palace in central India were the previous Raja had been a railway fanatic, and in the sumptuous banqueting hall he was shown a splendid small-scale steam railway which carried the food to and from the diners in the 1890s. The current Raja, a youngish politician and Minister in the government, talked with great pleasure on the railways and the past. He then interjected a standard ploy about the "exploitation" by the Brits of the Indian subcontinent. Sergeant looked at him with a challenging and friendly smile, and said, "Yes of course. They even took 5% per year profit." The Raja, a consummate politically correct politician, smiled back conspiratorially, twinkled his eyes, and said nothing

The point coming out of this is that time and again we hear this message, sometimes justified, about exploitation. It is a canon of the history which has been taught in our schools. But of course the 5% is a very low rate of return by any commercial standards.

So was it exploitation, or was it just normal trade and development, vital to India's and Britain's future?

*

Our next protagonist, **Jeremy Paxman,** is the widely admired television presenter of BBC's "University Challenge" (he's much loved by many students for taking the falsity out of politicians). He is admired particularly for the BBC Newsnight programme. On it he has famously challenged numerous public figures. Politicians like Michael Howard (a famous or infamous interview, depending how you see it, which is on the BBC website) to draw out the truth from their debates.

He is brought in here because his book *Empire* and its TV series are what people in the UK regard as an authoritative middle-of-the-road description and history of the Empire. To quote his recent TV series, he asserts that the Empire was "built on blood and a lust for power"[2]. I hope to show he had a lust for hokum! But he ends it in a much more admiring note.

He was born in Leeds in the North of England, educated at Malvern College and St Catharine's College Cambridge. There, significantly, he read English rather than history. Fiction rather than fact. He has had a long and distinguished career in journalism. Both the subject read and the career which followed tend to pull him to the personalities involved, militarism and the corridors of power, rather than the realities of history.

What is wrong with his book?

Like Simon Schama, he simplifies an extraordinarily complex subject by concentrating on a limited range of points of view. Schama gets his whole slant on the Empire by analysing the writings of George Orwell, derived from Orwell's short and unhappy service in the police in Malaysia or Burma, and the writings of Winston Churchill. Paxman makes much of Orwell's work, but goes in a much greater

---

[2] I believe I quote correctly – the programme is no longer on the BBC website. But I hope I'm wrong, and if I'm wrong I certainly retract.

depth on Churchill and his views from his time as a young adventurer and war reporter in South Africa and the Sudan right up to his death in 1965.

Churchill's was a massive and gripping opus, but very erratic and totally unrepresentative of the views of the Brits in this period. Still less of the actualities of empire.

What these guys should have done was to get at the actions and views of the people at the coal face. The District Commissioners, the Agricultural Officers and their Field Officers, and for the many other dramatically effective specialists from education through to mines, forestry, and every function of a modern state. It's important to get in touch with these old guys before they slip their moorings! Paxman did interview an ex-District Commissioner from Kenya. But the DC seemed like a wildebeest frozen in the headlights!

If we follow Paxman's fascinating book and the 30 pages at the back of references to printed sources, **not one** of the 600 references refers to debate with the people at the coal face. And they, as we will see later, were the ones who mattered. Even in the late 40s and 1950s, when the speed of communication between colonies and the UK are said in the conventional wisdom to have reduced the coal face to insignificance – automata driven from Whitehall – to quote Orwell as quoted in turn by Paxman **"well meaning men in dark suits and black felt hats, with neatly rolled umbrellas crooked over the left forearm, were imposing their constipated view of life on Ghana and Nigeria etc.**

The one time Empire builders were reduced to the status of clerks, buried deeper and deeper under mountains of paper and red tape."

*

The reality was that those "Empire (or Commonwealth) builders" at the coal face made nearly all of the key decisions as we'll see, and the myth that the politicians in Westminster and the governors at the top in the colonies made these decisions was nonsense. This we'll see throughout this book. In the Yemen for example, with regard to Denis Healey, (UK Foreign Office Minister) and the last Governor. When, at Independence, the Governor discussed with Healey what the Brits had achieved in Aden, he said "We taught them football and "fuck off" and bugger all else". But it wasn't like that, as I found when working there 25 years later, at the two British-originated Agricultural Research institutes. Much of the nation's key resource, agriculture[3], was founded on British research and innovation (from ARC (Agricultural Research Council) Rothamsted and its 13 research stations) – and links of affection and technology were still very live when I was there working for the UN's Food and Agriculture Organisation (FAO) in 1988. One of the great yens among the Yemeni research staff (and researchers throughout most of the Commonwealth) was to get a visit to "the Royal" (the Royal Agricultural Show) in Warwickshire! No matter that they came from a hot, dry, dusty desert environment – the Royal was their Nirvana. Perhaps rightly so, because it was a hub for much of the emerging technology and practice, as Maggie Thatcher told us firmly on our stand there in the eighties! Similar links are live and vital through most of the Commonwealth, and confound the critics.

No, the lives of the District Officers and their colleagues were immensely exciting, varied, adventurous, and dedicated, as we'll see later. It was a life involving tying your dog in the rest house for fear of the hunting leopard, coughing in the night in the gorge below. Or your Labrador persistently rolling in fresh elephant dung to disguise his scent, as happened with my friend Angus McCrae and his beloved "Dogge" as we'll see. Or your child nervously perched clinging over a cavernous pit latrine, the seat crafted for the imposing and vast posterior of Governor Sir Andrew Cohen.

---

[3] As the new boundaries in Arabia were being defined, the Yemen was described as "anywhere where there isn't any oil!".

Or for your local village being flattened by a herd of inebriated elephants, drunk from gorging on overripe fruits in the rainforest.

Graphic from photo, Sainsbury collection, British Museum.

That was not the life environment of paper-pushing clerks from London SW3 as Kapuscinski and Paxman would have us believe. It was a life of deep commitment. Of the twenty people I got to know well in Uganda, three lost closest relatives to the country. One a wife, one a brother, one a son. As a key instance of coalface initiative, one Agricultural Officer, still remembered affectionately twenty years later in Kigezi as "Bwana Fertility"(!), wrought a complete revolution in agriculture. A revolution for 500,000 people throughout a district the size of Yorkshire. And a revolution unnoticed by the UK Government. We'll see a similar pleasing divergence between what the guy on the ground was thought by UK HQ to be doing and the reality of what he/she really was doing when we look at Dianne Fossey. Isolated high up on the great Ugandan and Rwandan volcanoes, alone and lonely several years in the mists, bamboo, lobelia and giant groundsel, and the rare mountain gorillas of the heights. And among vicious poachers who eventually murdered her – but not till her mission had been achieved.

"Miss Fossey. You're supposed to be *studying* these mountain gorillas. What do you mean by saving their species from extinction? We may have to terminate your grant!"

I like to take readers on a voyage of exploration through many parts of the Commonwealth to try to pin down the benefits and drawbacks as I have seen in my twenty-one assignments and periods in the member countries.

The word "serendipity" was coined in English usage in 1754 by Horace Walpole, describing it from a Persian fairytale. It was used to tell, e.g., when an early explorer seeking spice producers in India suddenly came across the beautiful island of Ceylon, now Sri Lanka, where no island was expected. I'll follow a similar approach going through some of my various assignments, covering the achievements and failures I met. I hope this will give a piecemeal picture which in actual fact is rather characteristic of the Commonwealth.

Chapter 1
An Agricultural Revolution

When, from Kabale, in SW Uganda, you reached the Uganda/Rwanda border at Katuna in the 1950s you saw a startling contrast.

Across the half mile of lacustrine papyrus swamp in front, you saw in Rwanda that the steep hillsides were scarred by massive erosion, and usually carried no farmed vegetation. Only the narrow hill tops were cultivated, and often they were cultivated by Belgian settler farmers with large acreages of pyrethrum for DDT. DDT was then an approved insecticide to counteract malaria, and swiftly coming into general agricultural use as well. The local population, Banyaruanda, worked on the farms and cultivated small personal plots for subsistence food.

In striking contrast to this, the Ugandan hillsides were covered in "bunds", i.e. terraces. A typical bund was created by cutting down elephant grass and sods, and papyrus if close by, and laying it horizontally along the line of the hillside at perhaps forty foot wide strips This bunding was usually immediately effective in stopping erosion, and rainfall tended to build up the soil so that the bund was gradually reinforced and the strip flattened. Nothing compared with the immaculate rock-based horizontal terracing carved over centuries that you find in South East Asia, but nevertheless immensely effective and unknown in Uganda. Altering the slope can be tricky, and, as I remembered from research in Manchester, fine changes in the angle of slope could hit sudden thresholds. For example, over 13 degrees of slope was sometimes crucial. Getting the angle wrong could be dangerous, as for example in the disastrous land slip in Aberfan in Wales, when an entire school was engulfed, with appalling loss of the children buried under tons of mud.

Why the difference between Rwanda and Uganda?

The difference was largely created by one Agricultural Officer John W. Purseglove, when he first worked for three years in Kigezi. And also of course by the vigorous and receptive Kiga tribespeople and chiefs, who were later, happily, to escape the tragic slaughters carried out by Amin and Obote. For centuries, they had, like many mountain-dwellers, proved too hard a nut for autocrats, like in this case the Kabakas (kings) of Buganda, or recent Presidents Amin and Obote, to crack. And a source of innovation, individualism, and often fervent religious change. As the great historian Arnold Toynbee suggests, the ferment of civilisation tends to come from dwellers in the mountains, in the deserts and on the sea. Purseglove decided that the rapidly growing population (too much peace!) could only survive on the limited land available if there was a dramatic revolution in farming practices among the smallholders. He discussed this among the chiefs and councillors, and convinced them that change was essential, and recruited three experienced and well-trained white officers. "Extension" is the name of the advisory service[4] responsible for advising and enthusing farmers – we'll explore its importance later in discussing the Rubber Industry Smallholders' Authority in the eighties in Malaysia. Each of the officers was assigned to one of the key sazas or counties, and the revolution was started. A revolution which was to save the Ugandan peoples in Bufumbira from the appalling genocide – a million and a half people – of their tribal cousins across the border in Rwanda. He received an OBE in due course. Not for saving the 500,000 Bahutu and Watutsi from civil war and starvation (a rescue of which the UK Government in Whitehall were totally unaware!) – but for a later piece of research he carried out on taro in the West Indies. "Research" and "taro – a starchy root vegetable from South East Asia – *Colocasia esculenta*"[5] – now that's what he was supposed to be doing!

I'm following Purseglove's achievement now with three chapters covering my early experience as a fledgling District Officer to give readers an introduction to work in Uganda. Then we move on to the various groups who were introducing civilisation as we saw it where sixty years earlier it had been violent, brutish and short. Not my words, they were spoken by a leading West African historian, who was extracting from the philosophy of the 17th-century philosopher, Thomas Hobbes. "No arts; no letters; no society; and which is worst of all,

---

[4] Equivalent perhaps to the UK's ADAS (Agricultural Development Advisory Service), but with vastly greater responsibilities and authority.
[5] John Purseglove: A Pioneer of Rural Development. By E. Clayton. Ashford, Kent: Wye College Press (1993)

continual fear, and danger of violent death; and the life of man, (solitary), poor, nasty, brutish, and short."

Chapter 2

Beginnings

This chapter just gives family and personal backgrounds, and can be skipped. But take a look first at the lovely pictures from P&O! And the final paragraph.

As background, my story starts when I was three years old on a first voyage on my dad's ship – he was captain of the *Shahzada* in the Asiatic Steam Navigation Company's fleet (now P&O). We were moored in the Hoogly River, part of the Ganges, between Calcutta and Shalimar on the East bank near the famous botanical gardens. My granddad "Commander of the steamship *Rusinji*" used to catch the ferry across the river at Howrah to court my grandmother. On the ferry, a Bengali poet used to recite his version of English classics:

Kipling's splendid *Gunga Din*, and Tennyson's *Charge of the Light Brigade*:

Cannon to the rightside of them,
Cannon to the frontside of them,
Cannon to the leftside of them,
Cannon to the backside of them,
Volleyed and thundered.

This reflects our family's background – sealers and seafarers from the Orkneys, Shapinsay, in the farthest north of the UK,

POST-COLONIAL HOKUM

who roamed the world in the 18th and 19th centuries, and lived five generations under the British Raj in India.

I had never seen my dad before because we lived in the UK. But every 18 months his wife and children were allowed to join him on a voyage in the Far East. So the *Shahzada*'s bridge was really rather strange to me.

Graphic from "The story of the P&O".

On the bridge my dad pointed to a piece of rope on the end of which was a wooden ball, then lifted me up in his arms and said: "Graham, give a heave on that."

I grasped it, gave a heave, and the world fell apart, because the ship's whistle or siren was blasted off in a great cloud of steam. Not an experience people encounter nowadays, but believe me, to have that massive funnel sounding off within 30 feet of you left the whole bridge vibrating. No doubt I yelled and was comforted. It's the first event in my life I can remember.

After that came the Second World War, and my father shifted the family around the globe as the theatres of battle shifted between continents. First from Keston in the UK – "Vera, you wicked, wicked woman!" protested my aunt as my mother took us to Tilbury docks – then down Channel in the P&O liner Strathnaver through bomb alley on 13th July, 1940, the first day of the Battle of Britain. A raid started, and I was stuck with my sister under a table in the dining saloon. We were hit by a bomb but it failed to go off, perhaps thanks to saboteurs in Poland.

Graphic from "The story of the P&O".

On to Cape Town, then to Adam's Peak in Sri Lanka, thence by train to Bombay, now Mumbai, where we spent two happy years. It was nothing like as racist as is often portrayed. We had some Indian friends, Parsees, for example, with whom we got on well. Our block of flats had people from all races. But the only dark-skinned people I remember at Breach Candy swimming baths were the waiters.

Then in late 1941 the Japanese threatened India, so we upped sticks to St James, near Cape Town, RSA, where I had four years in the most wonderful environment for a young lad that can be imagined.

So my early upbringing gave me a taste inherited perhaps from my forebears for the wide, wide world and the Commonwealth.

There followed 10 years of education in an English public school, Hurstpierpoint, at Emanuel College Cambridge, and then a postgraduate year's training for the Colonial Service, on the Devonshire Course in Oxford. There, with two friends from Emma, I was trained in 1957 to go as a trainee administrator to Uganda.

This brings us to the training and background to the colonial service and leads in to the many assignments I had later overseas in the Commonwealth. It draws in much for example on agricultural research and production; on veterinary systems – how do you milk a cow in Zambia? On smallholder systems – how did 300,000 Malaysian smallholders produce 25% of the world's natural rubber? Computing for development, entomology – why don't we eradicate malaria? And so on.

What I would like to do is to deal with the subject areas and cite examples, so that readers are given a practical picture of the immensely exciting and satisfying life that development involved for me and my colleagues. Plus some very hazardous assignments, for example in the war zone of the Sudan, and as Agricultural Planning Consultant to Saddam Hussein in the build up to the first Gulf War, and then as a hostage.

All this will, I hope, start to discredit the view given by people like Schama, Paxman, and Kapuscinski.

In a nutshell, it's worth repeating, to borrow from current Potteries slang:

"They didn't been there. They didn't done that."

But we been there. We done that.

And so also done many others whom you will meet, and with many of whom I have been in contact throughout the last 50 years. We should build on these relationships round the Commonwealth, not destroy them.

Chapter 3

A New Recruit

In 1958, after a year's postgraduate training on the Devonshire Course at Magdalen College, Oxford, as a newly recruited District Officer (on 2 years' probation) I was posted to Uganda with two Cambridge friends. The journey out there was fantastic, three weeks at sea, and then disembarking in Mombasa, Kenya.

We left by train in the evening to wake up the next morning and see miles of open empty savanna rolling past – broad grasslands with scattered small trees – with giraffe, and herds of buffalo and kudu ignoring the train and grazing nearby. Then on up the flanks of the Great Rift Valley, which stretches from Arabia to Zambia. Over the Mau summit, the highest rail line in the Commonwealth, through Nairobi, then another night, to find ourselves at breakfast trundling through banana shambas and huts and into the Ugandan capital, Kampala. I bought a car, a splendid British-made Standard Vanguard estate, built like a tank with a Ferguson tractor engine, and set off with my wife, Alison, south-west to our district, Kigezi. First 80 miles of tarmac, delighting in our massive new (to us) car, to Masaka, and then on to the murrum surface, corrugated and potholed. A shattering experience – the car was rattling and banging, wearing out tyres, brakes, and shock absorbers, as it would for the next two years. The broad savanna gave way to great hills, like the English downs but higher, with narrow cloughs. They were lightly covered with beautiful red-flowered bottle brush trees, black-trunked Australian wattle, and the occasional jacaranda, drenched with beautiful blue flowers.

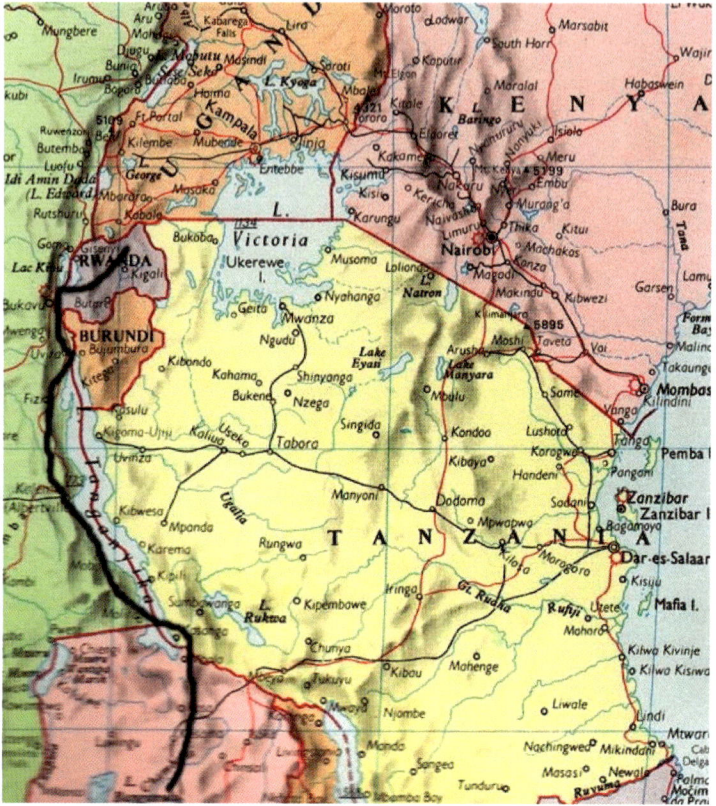

Hanging on the trees were occasional wooden beehives, small wooden barrels, waiting for people to collect honey (source of a much-prized liquor). Then another two hours winding through the hill country and we reached Kabale Township, our new home. The township was mostly located in a wide valley with a Catholic church a mile or so to the north-east and a Protestant church, the same distance to the south-west. Symbolising, as we'll see later, the main political division in the district between the Catholics, "Bakatoliki", and the Protestants, "Baprotetanti".

Graphic from Uganda Tourist Board.

Kigezi District is an astonishingly beautiful area, running down from 8-9,000 feet to the west to the vast empty game plains and savanna of the Rift Valley and Lake Edward at 2,000 feet. To the east a lovely "river lake" about twice the size of Windermere, called Bunyonyi, the "place of the little birds".

But on the dark side, in the 1850s Kigezi was the centre, as we'll see, of a growing, and savagely dangerous witch cult.

Witch graphic from Sainsbury collection, British Museum.

To the far east lay Tanzania and the great plains of Serengeti. Then over 50 winding, hair-pinned miles south (some officials from the capital refused to drive there) you go through bamboo forests at 8,000 feet and suddenly cross a summit to see Bufumbira. It's a beautiful saza (county) and towering above Bufumbira are the great southern volcanoes of Uganda: Muhavaura, 13,500 ft., the "rain-maker", roughly the height of the Matterhorn, Mgahinga, and Sabinio, the "old man", well-named, with a wizened, seamed face. In the great forests on the flanks are the famed mountain gorillas, in that time viewed as dangerous creatures fully capable of ripping humans to pieces. We'll see later how they were rescued from extinction.

The district of Kigezi (pronounced "chigezzi", the Bakiga pronounce leading **ks** as **ch**) was divided up into six sazas or counties, and in due course I was given responsibility for Bufumbira. It was inhabited partly by Bakiga but mostly by Bahutu and Batutsi, the same lethal mix of tribal peoples which was later to cause the appalling genocide, involving 1 million or more people, in Rwanda. How the same calamity was avoided in Uganda, I'll cover under agriculture.

We lived in attractive houses level with what was known as the Boma. Boma in many parts of Africa means a stockade, a protected area, sometimes protected by thorns. A standard rather divisive joke was that the Germans, who once governed modern Tanzania, had a zone 1,000 metres deep round each boma, where all vegetation was cut down to provide a field of fire for machine guns in case of an uprising of the people. The Brits achieved the same effect by creating fourteen splendid golf courses! I was to receive three reprimands during my service, one for failing to keep the golf course well-mowed, one for failing to keep the Union Jack in good nick, and one for mistakes in running Masindi Port Township (well merited).

In our case the Boma was an L-shaped block at the hill top with the offices for about 80 people. At one end the DC's office (District Commissioner) and his four ADCs, then the heads of the various key services like the DAO (District Agricultural Officer) the DVO (District Veterinary Officer), the CDO(W), the women's community development officer, the DMO (District Medical Officer), and so on. Some services had already been handed over to the local indigenous

Kigezi District Council – for example the responsibility for the district council roads and the local Gombolola and Saza Headquarters. With the council we were responsible for developing a district measuring about 80 miles by 40 with a million and a half inhabitants. And some magnificent fauna and flora.

Chapter 4

First Endeavours – Constitutional Development

Registrative Erections

The authority with which the district administrators were blessed was immense. For the first Legislative Council elections with secret ballot[6] ("Registrative Erections" some Bakiga were said to call them, because to the opposite of the Chinese, they don't sound the letter "l", keeping the tip of the tongue instead at the back of the palate. With the Chinese it's the letter "r"). In 1959 I, as a fledgling administrator, am charged with running the first election in Ruzhumbura County in Uganda. I have motored down the 60 miles out to the centre in my fine Standard Vanguard estate, and joined my team at the local rest house on the afternoon before polling. My team, already trained, includes the field officers and central government officers for the area. Special Branch have tracked down the cause of sudden massive buying of bicycle spokes by the Protestants. They were to be sharpened and used to prang ballot papers in the Catholic ballot boxes (with a hoe picture on the side) and transfer them to the Protestants' (with a car picture on the side). The slots have

---

[6] Previous elections had a simpler approach – you lined up behind the guy you supported and the chief counted the number in each line to get the result.

now rapidly been modified with a wooden lip to direct the papers sideways as in a UK post box. They can't be got out with the spokes. After finally discussing the procedures we settle down to a pleasant evening with roast chickens – kuku in Rukiga – and Nile beer. One of us is Fred Brown, the Fisheries officer, whom we will meet in his official role later on. He is a burly, big, bronzed, white Zimbabwean, rumour says a tractor driver unlike the rest of us who are formally qualified from university. He has been recruited for his experience in Africa. He is scared stiff of the possibility of an uprising at the election, and locks himself away in a storeroom all the night with a loaded shotgun.

Fast forward to 5am the next morning. The valleys are filled with voices of thousands of people on the move, and by dawn queues are forming in the local township and of course in many other stations throughout the saza. Catholics passionately against Protestants, and vice versa, each party aiming to get its people in first. By mid-morning I'm strolling with my interpreter in the hot, dry sunshine around the polling stations, the queues moving easily, good temper abounding and everything seeming to be going well. Both parties had mustered their voters out early in the hope of slowing the procedure and blocking the opposition supporters, but the procedure had been so practised by our officials that throughput has been swift. The township is a line of small shops and a Local Government office. And a prison. The rolling grasslands and hills surround us. And 30 miles to the West, crystal white against the clear monsoon blue, the Speke peak and glittering glaciers of the great range of the Ruwenzoris. The fabled "Mountains of the Moon" which had been rumoured to exist since the geographer Ptolemy in Roman times. But never seen by the "civilised world" until 1889. HM Stanley was here for three weeks in 1874 seeking them, but to no avail. Shrouded usually in cloud, craggy and unfriendly, their masses creating the great rainfall climate system, like a continental monsoon system which founds the environment of eight countries from the Congo round to Kenya.

Fred Brown, the Fisheries Officer, is in charge of the township polling stations. He strides up to me with the local candidate for the UPC and the Saza Chief, Paulo Kabagambe, the Gombolola Chief, the Muruka chief, a constable, and an askari holding a spear. The chiefs are in their brilliant white kanzus, their formal dress. The name, common through Africa, derives from the French "Quinze Aout", the 15th of August, the day commemorating and celebrating for the French the fall of the Bastille in the French Revolution in 1789. I'm in the uniform of an Assistant District Commissioner – starched khaki shorts, safari jacket with a single cord across the lapel, solar topee (sun helmet) with the golden Uganda Protectorate badge on the front.

Brown is taut and upset. He says that the local candidate has been addressing a meeting, which, as in most Commonwealth countries, contravenes the electoral law which bans political addresses on polling day. So he has placed the candidate under provisional arrest. I look up the ordinance, agreed with his action, and, as a second class magistrate, place the politician under full arrest. But, as we approach the prison a large, shiny, black official car draws up and out step six and a half feet of Provincial Commissioner. Bwana PC himself. The top, top man. He unfolds, complete with a prominent Adam's apple, a long, slender, tanned, horse-like face, and a bearing at once friendly and omniscient, conveying absolute, imperturbable, gentle, indisputable authority.

He is Sir George Duntze, Bart.

"How's it all going, Graham?" he asks. I explain.

He draws the candidate aside and talks quietly to him about the importance of these elections, the importance of an example to the people, the importance of appropriate behaviour by leading men like him who have such wide influence. The candidate, much flattered, agrees with immense deference. Sir George then says to us all: "I would like to set this incident aside, as part of the learning process for our great future. So we will take this matter no further."

The candidate is relieved. The chiefs and the askari are relieved, my interpreter is relieved, and even Fred is relieved. We are all relieved. They all leave us.

Sir George informs me alone and quietly: "Graham, the offence carries a 10 shilling fine!"

And I was about to put the politician in jail!

The Molson Commission and the Lost Counties

I resigned from the Protectorate Administration on Independence in 1962, although I was invited to stay on, because there was no stable future for a British administrator with a family of five to support, and the government was naturally committed to Africanisation.

My final posting as ADC Masindi – a semi-independent assignment – involved an event which I think of as being a high watermark of colonial rule.

The development of Uganda from the 1890s was bedevilled by what came to be known as the Lost Counties Dispute.

When the whites first came to this region in the 1850s two kingdoms dominated the area – Bunyoro, longstanding but overstretched empire, and Buganda, up-and-coming, civilised, and superbly administered by the standards of the area. Men like Speke, Grant, and later Thruston, approaching from the East, achieved a close working relationship with the Kabaka, or king of Buganda, whereas Kabarega, the ruler of Bunyoro, fought bitterly against explorers like Samuel Baker[7] coming down from the North. (The history of Kabarega's fight against Sir Samuel Baker and his Sudanese mercenaries is inspiring. He lost the battle of Masindi, as shown, but by guerrilla tactics drove Baker's force away sixty miles to the north, and fought for many years.)

---

[7] Sir Samuel Baker and his formidable wife Florence explored towards the great Lakes from the North for the Egyptian government. It makes a fascinating story and the impression made in the area by Lady Baker, fully dressed in Victorian rigout and bustles, on Africans who had never seen the like was prodigious. One of the Bakers' techniques in impressing the chiefs involved some large electric batteries. Sir Samuel would hold the leads in both hands with no evident distress, then hand them to the leading chief. As the chief took the terminals Lady Baker pressed a plunger, and the chief was significantly impressed.

THE BATTLE OF MASINDI
From Baker's Ismailia, 1874

So the Brits worked with the Kabaka and proceeded with the conquest of Bunyoro. In due course the Protectorate Government imposed 62 years' peace in the area, and the boundaries of the constituent counties were assessed and ratified. But the close relationship between Buganda and the Protectorate Administration meant that many key jobs including the chieftains and the interpreters, were assigned to Baganda, and as the county boundaries were debated, the Baganda interpreters translated the evidence to their compatriots' benefit. So vast numbers of Banyoro were forced to live under the alien Baganda (alien language, clashing culture, antipathetic), despite their intensely felt allegiance to their old Kingdom and its[8] heroic king, Kabalega.

The Lost Counties Dispute festered throughout the British Protectorate, and the area as I experienced it was afflicted with apathy as a result. The contrast with Kigezi was striking and shocking. Development was lethargic and the people apathetic. And yet the chiefs retained immense power. I

---

[8] Kabalega fought and evaded capture for many years before he was taken and exiled to the Seychelles. He was returned eventually, to die tragically as he was about to cross back into his realm.

remember giving a baraza before the elections on the importance of registration and participation. In Kigezi the process had been popular and immaculate. We even had polls of over 100% – sons voting with their recently deceased fathers' slips.

But here in Bunyoro, the saza chief, the Kaigo, entered the meeting, massive, heavy, gowned and menacing, and my interpreter froze stiff with incoherent terror. I repeated my previous sentence quietly, then again, and the interpreter recovered and translated.

"You support this election?" I asked the Kaigo.

"My people will do what they will do."

I should add that some of the leaders of the Banyoro were immensely able and courageous. Notably the Katikiro, effectively Prime Minister, grandson of the great King Kabarega and trained in the UK in agriculture and with a successful career, eventually DAO, District Agricultural Officer, in the Agricultural Department before becoming Prime Minister. I well recall his speech to a vast concourse at the evening opening of the Mukama's new Palace.

"As for you, our British friends, I fear you are leaving too soon. But the next ten years will tell." And so, tragically, they did, with the massacres and tortures under Presidents Amin and Obote. I particularly liked the Katikiro's deputy, with whom we used to play tennis at the Hoima club. He had picked up his tennis skills when studying in the UK – Oxford I think – in the thirties, notably the chop. "Chop!" he would shout with pleasure, and slice the ball viciously so that it glided over the net and barely kissed the ground. Unplayable.

The Colonial Office, advised by the governor Sir Frederick Crawford, resolved that this Lost Counties Dispute, a festering sore, needed to be cured as independence approached. So the Molson commission, consisting of three QCs – Lord Molson, the Earl of Listowel and one other were appointed by the UK ministry and came out to Masindi.

The District Commissioner, Keith Arrowsmith, set arrangements in hand, and we met the three QCs at the Railway Hotel (the railway's nearest point was a hundred miles away – it served the river and lake steam ships) and took them in two Land Rovers without their usual drivers way away from overhearing into the forests. We reached a place where, as in tribal practice, three massive trunks were laid out in a triangle to sit on, for tribal elders' barazas. Sandy ground, a large clearing, scattered tall forest trees, probably muvule[9] (the first branches typically a hundred feet up), a warm African morning, chilled Nile beers with sandwiches at lunch. It was absorbing and very British. Keith was quizzed about the royal and tribal background, and administrative structure, social anthropology, legal procedures, agriculture and industry, etc. Once Keith was stumped, and said with a characteristic, engaging, lop-sided smile: "Sorry chaps, haven't done my homework on that one."

The Commission went ahead with taking on interpreters, stenographers and so on, and arranging hearings and depositions throughout the disputed counties. It was a very lengthy and absorbing process, and eventually the Molson report was published in Uganda and the UK. The commission recommended the return from Buganda to Bunyoro kingdom of three of the eleven "lost" counties, and, because of the long,

---

[9] Milicia excelsa A superb hardwood rather like teak, specially useful because it is resistant to termites. Replanting campaigns are run in many villages under the Mvule project in 2000. Called the "Gold of Busoga". Harvested massively – I remember coming across one on safari in the jungle, felled, and one strong man on top and another in a pit underneath, heaving up and down at a rip saw to cut it into planks. Modern propaganda asserts that "the British couldn't be stopped from taking the trees" and exported them But in fact the Local Government charged a fee of £50 per tree, and the foresters sold the planks wherever they could find a market.

friendly, quiet thoroughness and formality of the exercise,[10] this met with reasonable popular approval in both kingdoms.

However, the crunch came – would the commission's recommendation be accepted? We all assumed yes. But the British cabinet decided that, with independence approaching, the risk of massive civil, perhaps armed, dissent was too great and deferred the matter to be decided by the independent government. A massive mistake, I feel personally, because the Lost Counties issue exploded in due course and resulted in a breakdown of government. I'd add that this explosion, and the tragedy of Amin's misrule and the massacres of half a million Ugandans is not attributable to the Colonial Office. As Independence approached, the Colonial Governor and his deputies had struck up a friendly and easy-going relationship with the incoming administration, led by Milton Obote. Much as occurred with immense success in India (Mountbatten and Nehru) or Ghana (Arden[11] Clarke and Kwame Nkrumah). Once the Union Jack fell and the Ugandan flag was raised, this relationship was ruthlessly chopped by the incoming UK Foreign Office officials in the High Commission. And they were the incompetents who supported Amin's coup d'etat eight years after independence. This despite the long record of excessive brutality in his previous career.[12] For the UK FO,

---

[10] Not to mention the Lords! A Queen's Council is a title not to be trifled with. Nor I believe, is the House of Lords.

[11] Brian Lapping UK Channel 4 Book End of Empire pp 376 et ff.

[12] Amin in Karamoja. Karamoja on the North Eastern Frontier of Uganda with Kenya was by far the least developed area of the Protectorate. A friend described how when he went to the office for the first time he was impressed by his immaculately dressed interpreter - sharply creased shorts and well ironed kaki government shirt. He was even more impressed when at the end of work the clerk removed all his clothes except his shoes and strode off homewards stark naked.

The local tribal custom was for younger men to blood their spears by raiding across the border, killing and wounding the Masai and carrying off their cattle. This was a necessary preliminary to full

Amin was a soldier, a sound, reliable NCO by background, who came up through the ranks in the KAR – Kings African Rifles – much preferable to a left-wing inclined President like Obote.

*

Let's move back from the first stage in democratic government with secret balloting as I encountered it as a trainee in 1958, to the situation in Uganda as it was found by the early explorers, army officers, and missionaries. Fraught with danger from an unpredictable tyrant – Speke was held at the Kabaka's court by Mutesa for three months, and nineteen early converts in his court to Christianity were martyred – after a long and immensely dangerous and difficult journey from the coast, and the murder of the first Bishop Hannington as he approached from the East.[13]

*

I think we should turn now to our next protagonist, to one

---

manhood and getting married. As a sergeant-major, Amin was sent to get this under control, and one of his techniques was to call a meeting at the gombolola headquarters. There he would call the local chief to stand opposite him by the table on the customary raised stage in full view of the people. Amin would have a sharp panga in his hand and raise it up. He would order the chief to open his fly buttons – no plastic zips in those times – and lay his member on the table. He would then lower the panga and warn the chief what would happen if the capital raiding did not cease. This practice is known in industry in the UK as putting your cock on the block. But I have not heard of it being used quite so literally.

[13] The Baganda believed that their forbear, a man named Kintu, a white-skinned man, came from the East and created their state, before departing to the West. And that his destined successor, also white would approach from the East. So they murdered the white bishop lest he be Kintu's successor. Some historians suggest that the original white man was a Portuguese who had been shipwrecked near Mombasa and was trying to get back to his homeland.

of the most influential of the Empire's critics, a maverick socialist Member of Parliament, Tony Benn. He was for 50 years a prominent left-wing speaker, a splendid orator, and with an astonishing feel for an audience on BBC programmes like Question Time. He had a distinguished time as Harold Wilson's Minister for the re-vamping of British industry. For example, he engineered a merger between Britain's three main computer firms to form International Computers Ltd. And that firm had an immensely effective development history until the government permitted its takeover by an ailing industrial giant, Standard Telephones and Cables. A precious seed corn which most countries would have fought to protect and the Japanese firm Fujitsu eventually acquired – relevant to the discussion of industrial development later in the book. He also produced numerous appealing but wacky ideas – for example that pensioners from Newcastle should travel 250 miles to London on British rail for free to fill up the space available on the trains. It went down well in political shows, until you got back home and thought about it.

One of his main targets was the Empire, and I wrote to him challenging them and his reply follows in the end-of-chapter footnote.[14]

---

[14] *Dear Mr. Tottle,*
I was very interested indeed to read your letter and I hope you will not think that in my comments on imperialism I was querying the high quality, commitment and dedication of those who worked in the Colonial Office or in the colonies themselves.
I know many who did what you have done and respect you for it.
But I do not believe that British imperialism was motivated by Christian charity or designed to help the poor benighted natives.
Of course there was savagery in Africa but since Europeans killed 50-60 million people in two world wars we are not exactly an example of high standards ourselves.
All empires were built because of the power it gave, the raw materials it provided and the market for its goods.
For example, when I was in Zimbabwe during the war, then called Rhodesia

But for our present purpose, how sensible was his conclusion that in all cases democracy must reign paramount? How on earth would one have gone about setting up democracy in Uganda in the 1890s? We have just seen that a successful initial entry into democracy was achieved as shown in my description of the first secret ballot elections in Uganda, 1958. But that was after 60 years of astonishing development in every aspect of human society.

Let's now see Buganda in the 1890s and assess how credible Tony Benn's view is. The first British explorers to reach Buganda were astonished to find that in place of the scruffy kraals and the ill-defined tracks through dry bush which characterised inland East Africa in many parts; there were wide straight thoroughfares on dark red earth, verged by green grass, running up hill and down dale between lush, neatly cultivated gardens. The houses were sharply thatched with the same thick papyrus reed thatching which looks so good on ancient Egyptian and Meroitic murals, and the people were finely dressed in soft, beaten bark cloth from bark stripped off the mutuba tree, in place of smelly part-cured hides you found elsewhere.

"As they approached along by the lake, there was ever-growing evidence of civilisation, till they reached the capital on a hill-top. It was a sort of palace which started with a wide ring of outer huts surrounding a regal centre. And here they found crowds strolling around, the women bare to the waist, in soft brown skirts, the men in long toga-like gowns, 'recalling the saints, the Blessed walking in Paradise', as the explorer Harry Johnston put it."

"And there they reached the 'worm i' the bud', the Kabaka, with an incredibly obsequious entourage of nobles, wives, a

---

with 6 million Africans who had no vote and the farmland having been stolen from the Matabele and Mashona by Rhodes himself.
Nor should we forget the very profitable slave trade which we organised.
With very kind regards.

hundred or more, page boys and slaves."

Back to the worm in the bud, Sabassajja the Kabaka; in 1862, the young King Mutesa II. The court was reminiscent of that of the French Roi Soleil, Louis XIV, the Sun King, with the same pomp and ritual attending his every function. But whereas in France, the King's displeasure was metaphorical death, in Buganda it was actual death, often under excruciating and very audible torture.

The King would promenade, striding like a rampant lion, stiff-legged, over the grasses, in a blue and white check dress, his face covered sometimes in white war paste.

A massive crowd would be in admiring attendance. If he stopped to speak the crowd would wait in tense silence. When he stopped speaking, they would throw themselves to the ground uttering strange cries. "Yanziga! Yanziga!" *He has said it! He has said it!* Dissent of course was unthinkable, but even the most trivial error in ritual brought death. If the King bethought himself to sit, one of the pages, as for Queen Victoria, had to get a seat in place to anticipate the royal bottom. But in this case the seat was the page himself, crouched on his knees, and for a minor error he would be dragged off screaming to execution. Heads were lopped off with casual indiscriminacy, and terror was the predominant feature of the state. At the first meeting with Speke, the Kabaka demanded his rifle. Speke demurred, and then when things looked ugly, gave in. Mutesa handed the gun to someone, and gave a command. The rifle holder went outside, ordered someone to run, drew a bead on his head, waited a bit, and shot him dead. This met with wild admiration.

Much has been written about the economy, culture, and politics of Buganda then. A general conclusion was that the state was dedicated to the pursuit of ivory, slaves, and war as described, e.g., by AB Thruston.[15]

---

[15] The accounts of the horrors of the Kabaka's court. Written

But the clincher arises from hobbyists in genealogy. It's a hobby now among many Baganda as with most people. But they face difficulties – you can never be sure, for the times before Uganda's pax Britannica, or as Graham Greene called it, the great Victorian peace, that great-great-great Uncle Fred really was great-great-great Uncle Fred. Not for the reasons you'd expect, e.g. no birth registration records, because the Baganda can often trace the generations back, even in some cases to the 16th century. The line of progenitors was a matter of keen verbal record, passed down from father to son. Abraham begat Isaac, and Isaac begat Jacob and so on. A reason perhaps why they like the Old Testament so much.

---

by men like Speke, Stanley, and Grant, the authorities are Speke, Emin Pasha, Apollo Kagwa, and Brevet Major AB Thruston. He particularly, because he was a clear-eyed guy with little sympathy with regimental life, jingoism, and the Victorian imperial attitudes of his time, and a deep love of Africa. He was killed eventually by the Banyoro, who rightly saw him as a threat to their kingdom and culture. See *African Incidents* by he and his brother, published by John Murray, Albemarle St London, 1900.

Were these accounts all fabrications? Highly improbable if you study their diaries.

Graphic from "African Incidents" Brevett Major AB Thruston, John Murray, 1900.

No, the difficulty arises because of the terrifying nature of the Kabaka's court. As with medieval European courts, the top barons were obliged to send their first-born, or at least one of their sons, to court. To pick up the flavour; training and experience and so on. Also as hostages for the baron's dutiful subservience.

But because of the hazards, many barons used to send, not their sons, but a scion of some lesser guy, going along to the court with the son's name, as Fred, or Bisamunyu or whoever. So tracking back to great-great-great Uncle Fred has to take account of this major fault in the records. Did Abraham really beget Isaac? As a Malaysian might say, who can tell?

I dwell on this history in detail because it is fundamental to the views of Benn and most other critics of Empire. Tony Benn is clearly way off course. Not until 60 years of colonial and cultural development and the first election described earlier was it sensible to talk of democracy in Uganda.

*

One of my first introductory, training, safaris was to go to Kisizi at the centre of Rukiga County and join Mike Purcell, ADC1, and Tom Ellis, who ran local extension services. A gaunt, muscular, knobbly kneed Agricultural Field Officer, Major Tom Ellis, a key guy, one of the few who as a Japanese Prisoner of War survived the notorious Japanese "Railway of Death". (Beautifully described in the film *Bridge over the River Kwai*.) We'll meet him later in the book; suffice it to say for the present that I arrived in Kigezi a reasonably good cross-country runner fit from training around Oxford. But keeping up with him and the chiefs and Agricultural Assistants as they toured the hillside villages between six and nine thousand feet had me really creased at first.

I arrived there in the evening in a rest house by the Kisizi hospital, run by one of the Sharps. It had been built there with powerful symbolism to counter the existing tribal practices, often barbarous. For example, if a young woman became pregnant without first being married, she was sentenced by the elders to be carried to the hundred foot cliffs above the Kisizi waterfall, for her father to throw her over the fall to her death.

I joined them for dinner, preceded by Nile lager, feeling

like a new boy at school first dining with the prefects. The boy ("boy" was the commonly used term, in no way pejorative) brought in a splendid roast chicken (pronounced in Rukiga "cuckoo") – a real treat for me, used to the more restrained and flavour-free birds in the UK. I dug in with zest, hoping for a second helping, but Mike rang the bell and it was whisked away.

The next morning we piled into Land Rovers with chiefs and Assistant Extension Officers, drove to Rubale, then left the vehicles to start climbing into the hills. As we passed the farms, we would sometimes inspect/visit them. Into the main hut – was the thatching sound, was provision made for the smoke to get out, was there provision below the thatch outside for water run-off, etc.? Then the kitchen and latrines. I remember twenty years later in a health baraza of about 300 Banyoro by a Health Director in Hoima. "When the Bazhungu (whites) were here 80% of you had latrines. Now only 20%. How come? Who were you building the latrines for? For you or for the whites?"

It got a splendid laugh.

Continuing our safari, we then inspected the famine reserve. This was a very tall – eight foot – conical container, made with woven grass sides, and raised on stilts to keep rats out. As in many parts of Africa, the famine reserve was usually of finger millet. Not a tasty cereal compared with maize or sorghum, so that people were not tempted to eat it, and it lasted for years. In West Africa, black cassava was often an alternative famine reserve. Containing, I think, arsenic, and poisonous unless boiled – and not therefore eaten by rodents. The rules about famine reserves were applied by us with particular emphasis, and in my five years in Uganda, famine supplies had only once to be brought in from outside, in Masindi in the North West. I remember, as I ran the distribution, commenting caustically on the content, which included hundreds of tins of Heinz baby food but no tin openers, and crates of bottles of Kraft salad cream. The salad cream may have been nutritious and welcome flavouring for the posho (boiled maize flour), but the tins of baby food rapidly reappeared on sale in the local markets. My comments were typical of the scepticism of youth, because I spent most of my time supervising the disbursement of truckloads of maize flour – vital, welcome nutritious, and in wide demand. That was what mattered.[16]

The visits were accompanied by much cheery laughter, and we gave most attention to the quality of maize and coffee cultivation. The smallholders could get healthy root-pruned Arabica from the Department's seedling nurseries, and it

---

[16] Famine. A recent EIR report states hilariously that the British Raj deliberately generated a famine every two years throughout its history to ensure that the population were kept under control I come from a family of five generations who served in India, and I find this very difficult to reconcile with the evident pride and commitment which they seemed to show. More importantly than that, I think, is the succession of historical novels by John Masters about a family called Savage and the description of their experience and work in India eg in "The Nightrunners of Bengal". His family background is very similar to mine, and his commitment is much deeper. One academic quote I find particularly convincing:
British authorities began to discuss famine policy soon after the Orissa famine, and, in early 1868, Sir William Muir, Lieutenant-Governor of Agra Province, issued a famous order stating that:"every District officer would be held personally responsible that no deaths occurred from starvation which could have been avoided by any exertion or arrangement on his part or that of his subordinates."
My deduction, for what it's worth, is that the Government's policy on famine management as a conflict between compassion on the one hand and the prevalent laissez-faire economics of the time, affected greatly by the writings of Malthus, John Stuart Mill and Darwin. This general area is absorbing but not in the scope of this book. I'm concerned primarily with that about which I can write with personal knowledge, and famine prevention was central to imperial policy then.

needed careful replanting at standard intervals and regular weeding, fertiliser, and in the rainy season spraying with Benlate, a copper-based fungicide at two-week intervals to control CBD (coffee-berry disease).

By the afternoon you were pretty tired, particularly if you were a follower, with Ellis and Purcell leading the intercourse with the chiefs and farmers. Then we reached the meeting area for the baraza with the local people. Often great fun, with perceptive questions – why do we have to pay tax twice, on our poll tax, and then again when we buy cigarettes or paraffin? What sense is there in paying the opposition Members of Parliament? You will just encourage them to oppose. As I picked up Rukiga, the local Bantu language, I got used to letting the interpreter do his task while I had time to prepare an answer. "No," I might eventually reply challengingly, to a quickening of attention. "Ngaha." – No – James would translate with a dramatic emphasis, getting a quickening of interest. Then I'd give a cogent reason for the "No," and James would put it across. The interpreters were key guys, usually good and persuasive communicators. I remember once James Nyagahima interrupting when traditional marriage procedures were at issue.

Surely, I said to him (from a young liberal's point of view), we should let these customs stay?

"Mr Tottle," he replied, "have you read about these customs?"

I hadn't. I did. He was right.[17]

---

[17] Mary M. Edel, *The Chiga of western*, Uganda. The anthropologist describes the fascinating and sometimes abominable and violent rituals in traditional Chiga marriages on pages 52-57. International African Institute, OUP 1957.

Chapter 5

Industrial Development

I'd like to break in here, now there is a feel for Kigezi, to fill in on the training we had at Oxford.

The Devonshire Course

We joined the course for colonial administrators confident that it would be a doddle. An upper second degree from Emanuel College Cambridge, you can't get better than that! Our first degree courses were based on the Oxbridge pattern of a weekly tutorial. A one-to-one session with your tutor on your essay, a list of references to base your next week's work on from the Seeley historical library, and lectures from the leaders in current historical research if you so wished. Otherwise do as you wish. And so we did.

But the Devonshire Course was something different. The range of subjects is shown below, usually also from the readers in their subjects, and with demanding exams in each before you would qualify as a trainee administrator. And a wife to support! Wives were welcomed to attend the lectures.

Language – Luganda, taught by R.A. Snoxall, with great emphasis on correct grammar and also on social interaction and pronunciation, in sessions with two Baganda advisors among a group of six of us.

Law – English laws of crime and of evidence.

Agriculture and veterinary science – training by Masefield, an expert in tropical agriculture.

Agricultural economics – training by a guy who had built up an estate in Tanzania growing sisal – hard experience, and eventual failure. The Tanzanians didn't enjoy sisal harvesting!

Ecology – a word I had never heard before, and the training was invaluable background for me in persuading the tribespeople that cutting down the bamboo forests above their plains in Bufumbira could destroy their underground water supplies.

Local government – training in the theory, and a fortnight's practical experience with a local authority.

Trade Union law – ADAS dispute procedures etc.

History – demanding group sessions where you had to present your ideas, covering the history of East and Central Africa by the Oxford historian who had been covering it from pre-historic times to the present. Dame Margery Perham, among the most famous historians of the colonies, was then at St Hughes and I think gave one of the lectures.

Medicine – theory and practice with tropical diseases, including taking blood samples and studying them under a microscope to see if they contained the malarial parasite.

Social anthropology – studying the behaviour patterns of the tribes we expected to serve. Marriage rituals for example, and the social systems which held together the clans and tribes in the southern Sudan.

Survey – we were taken out to the green grasses of the park equipped with pegs, posts, cords and theodolites and required to layout for levelling a tennis court for our new station.

The range was demanding and fascinating. Even in the survey, which we found a hoot. Which of us would ever need all this? Setting up a tennis court? And when I got to my posting, what was the foremost need? To understand and support with the local people just such a survey activity. The team at the top of a 13,000 foot volcano was triangulating to cover the entire plain up to 10 miles away in tiny plots, each often less than a tenth of an acre. Immensely sensitive of course, as was anything to do with landownership – a rich breeding ground for turbulent agitators.

Quite a course, and it had been training administrators since 1925. The picture from Rhodes House archives shows a group photo from one of the first courses. To assess the impact of these people and their history would be fascinating, but the details are lost.

Graphic from Rhodes House, Bodleian Library, Oxford.

The Township Labour

Our training on the Overseas Services course at Oxford involved a two-week assignment to a local district authority, in my case West Malling District Council in Kent. I found it fascinating, and was particularly impressed with their high-tech milk pasteurisation system. It involved the milk cascading through stainless steel cladding like a waterfall so that having been heated to 70° it was then rapidly cooled to zero or so, thereby ensuring pathogenic microbes were destroyed. But in Kigezi things were different. The milk was brought round every morning in a beautifully hand-turned container of mvule, a local hardwood, finely grained, similar to mahogany but much heavier. A very thick, curved bottom to the container, thickest at the centre, so that it always rolled upright rather than capsizing and emptying.

Author's photo.

This was sterilised, so we were told, by peeing into it – your pee is antiseptic. Though smoking is also possible. A different approach to that in West Malling, though when boiled (as it always was) the cream on the top was thick and delicious. The local dairy cattle, the Asiatic Zebu, imported, I think, by the Brits from Southern Sudan or Egypt, were renowned for this. The indigenous Ankole Longhorns, brought south in the 13th century by Hamitic tribes such as the Batutsi, had long been bred for their size and extraordinary horn-spread. They related to the monarch, the Omukama – the Princess was as filled with the milk as a French goose with corn for pâté de foie gras, and she was appallingly fat as a symbol of the Kingdom's wealth and prosperity. So fat that the ADC, designated to help her ceremonially into the royal apartment in the opening of the first ever railway train, had to get help and was violently sick afterwards. The Ankole Longhorn cattle were very poor milkers and deeply subject to tuberculosis. Anyway, the West Malling approach involving heavy machinery and mains electricity for the pasteurisation of the milk clearly didn't fit at all. To borrow from the jargon, it was not "appropriate technology", as we'll see in Chapter 12.

However, the sewage system seemed to me a better bet, and I, as the junior ADC, ADC 4, was in charge of administering the township of about 4,000 people. The sewage was collected nightly, as in Manchester in the 1850s, by night-soil men numbering about 60. They went to each house in the dark, put the excrement bucket on their heads and walked down to the tip, half a mile away, tipped it into the pit and returned for the next and so on. But this was the 20th century, I felt – we must modernise. So I had a large tank, eight feet by three by six, with a hatch, built onto a trailer by Kartar Singh at the local garage, and this would be pulled round the town so that the night-soil could be tipped in house by house. Pulled possibly by a bullock. All in a single trip right round the town. Despite advice from Bazhungu, the Township Headman, I decreed the new system be put into operation two weeks before Christmas. We had to progress. We were in the second half of the 20th century, I explained. There was an immediate protest by all the night-soil men, leading to a strike a week before Christmas. Not a pretty prospect. I held a baraza with them in the township lines (we had been taught on the Devonshire Course about industrial practice, ACAS (Advisory and Conciliatory and Arbitration Service) and negotiation procedures in the UK). The night-soil force objected to my system because, they said, it humiliated them. Under the old approach they went around in the dark, from midnight on. Under the new approach they would work in broad daylight, and people, especially the children, would scoff and jeer. So they were going on strike. At the prospect of a strike and no toilets cleared over Christmas the entire township, as you can imagine, were furious.

In the end my boss, ADC1, Mike Purcell, radioed one of the white hunters, Manoli Fangoudis, a bronzed thick-set Greek with a limp from a buffalo wound – buffalo are the most feared of the big game, wound one and it will lie and hide in wait for you and wreak its revenge – down on the game plains eighty miles away, now the Queen Elizabeth Park. He shot and sent us four buffalo (from many thousands). We had reconciliation discussions, followed by a grand ox-roast in the township labour lines on Christmas Eve, and the new high-tech approach was accepted. My first ox-roast. Thirty years before they became fashionable. I should have probed for significant redundancies among the night-soil men since the workload was reduced by 90%. But I didn't.

I revisited Kabale in the eighties and again in the noughties to see old haunts and the wonderful lakes and mountains – it's now the centre of 90% of the nation's tourist trade. A great pleasure to find the massive borrow pits from which the roads were surfaced with murrum, which I'd designated as the municipal park, really was now a real park, trees blazing with Flame of the Forest and a line of Jacaranda trees in blossom, blue as the sky. The Second Class Housing Area, which I'd inaugurated off under instructions from the capital, looked good. We had insisted on dipping the first foot of all wall stakes or posts in a drum of really hot creosote to deter termites and this had worked a treat. For fifty years.

Like all Uganda's "stations" – i.e. townships – Kabale had had a wonderful nine-hole golf course, venue for international tournaments. This was now in 2009 like a vast unkempt hay field. Acres of previously immaculate greens rolling round and among copses, by the famous White Horse Inn. This had been run by a formidably strict Austrian lady, Gytha Calder. A commonplace among the Brits was that the Germans had created a 1,000-metre circle round each of their stations as a killing area, which could be commanded by automatic machine guns in case of rebellion. The Brits achieved the same effect with our golf courses – whether intentionally I know not. Probably not. This brings to mind a comment from Kofi Annan when I was with him in Iraq:

"If your plane's brought down somewhere in Africa how do you know which imperialists ruled it? If it was the French you'll be surrounded with vegetables. If the Brits you'll be surrounded with flowers."

The unroofed squash courts we'd built from the old prison were in reasonable nick, but never used and a tree with a foot-thick trunk had burst through the wall halfway up, and flourished like the green bay tree.

Sika Qualcrete

Let's fast-forward from early urban/industrial development in 1959 in Uganda to industrial development forty years later, to a key firm in India's fast-thriving industry, Sika Qualcrete . It's a good example of the value of cross-Commonwealth collaboration.

In 2000 I was assigned to this firm in Calcutta at the request of Bhaskar Sen, its MD, to provide a month's consultancy and direction to their computing systems. This was organised by the UK's British Executive Service Overseas, who targeted professionals with long experience who could advise organisations where needed. Sika produce the high-tech adhesives, additives, and general structural bonding materials used in nearly all their major dams, bridges, and civil engineering. Vital to their infrastructure and economy. You felt a surge of pride as you drove on the great motorway bridge over the Ganges, Vidyasagar Setu. I helped do that! My dad and his dad used to anchor their ships upstream by Howrah.

*

Baskar Sen's history is absorbing. At the time of the partition[18] between India and what became Pakistan he lived in the Muslim area, now Bangladesh, member of a prominent and very wealthy Hindu family. His father had been a leading opponent of the British Raj, and had had spells of imprisonment by the Brits. Baskar worshipped his father and longed, like him, to take on the Brits. At the partition in August 1947, violence and massacre broke out as the Muslim and Hindu populations – perhaps a million people fled to cross the frontiers to their fellow religious peoples. As a Hindu, he had to abandon all and flee with his family, clambering onto a massively crowded train, destitute.[19] There in Calcutta (or Kolkata) he managed to gain scientific training, and eventually set up his own manufacturing company to produce the chemicals. A remarkable triumph over adversity. He recruited a

---

[18] For an absorbing account of the partition see *Partition and its Legacies* by Dr Crispin Bates. For a splendidly biased anti-British polemic try the Marxist "The 1947 Partition" and "India under the British Boot". Both on Wikipedia.

[19] He blamed not Mountbatten, but Pandit Nehru, the leader and eventual Prime Minister, who should have agreed to serve under the Muslim, Jinna, for the sake of the country's peace and unity.

very able team of managers and gradually his firm came to dominate their sector.

Despite his radical past, Baskar had great affection for Brits and British culture, and I had occasional dinners with him and his management team at which he would hold forth especially on the virtues of cricket as a key means of developing the character traits needed for successful managers and scientists. (Near to my own heart – though I remember one Ugandan cricketer who enthused about Hitler! "Who had the right ideas.") We met in Calcutta, many people of similar backgrounds, and were often entertained in the various clubs, most having a pleasing, friendly similarity to the clubs in London – leather settees, fine panelled walls, beautiful parquet floors, cigar smoke, pictures of the Indian countryside and of prominent past members sometimes on the walls. Best of them was the Tolley Club, placed unbelievably near to the city centre and including a beautiful eighteen-hole golf course and superb gardens of many rare plants. I had the great pleasure of living there and found the history fascinating. The buildings were originally assigned as a palace for the heirs, after Wellesley killed him, of their great enemy, Tippoo Sahib[20] of Mysore, a sympathetic way of defusing corrosive resentment. They had a pleasing regal splendour. The area was embellished with some lovely large fish and lily ponds, and a quarter-mile long avenue for tent-pegging. This is a sport in which the Indians and the Brits often enjoyed and where there was considerable military significance. The partaker sits astride his horse with a spear in his hand and thunders down the avenue until he approaches the tent peg, then hangs out from the saddle to try to spear it and carry it up and away. To stand alongside as the horse and rider thunder down, thrust the spear and pass, is a lovely

---

[20] Tippoo waged heroic campaigns against the Brits, a formidable leader who dramatically developed his administration in Southern India and was eventually killed by Wellington's army in the fourth Mysorean War, which was to establish the British Raj.

experience. Civilisation and relative luxury compared with the grinding poverty all around.

I paint this picture to give you an idea of the closely similar features of Indian and British industry, society and culture – long may the relationship prosper. Through Joint Ventures, common accounting conventions, etc. Notable for example in the architecture, not so much in Calcutta's great white Victoria Memorial but in the famous Writer's Building, some of the finest colonial architecture there is, and for neo-Gothic buildings like the Scottish Presbyterian church where my grampa and grandma were wed in 1892 – now the Nepalese Anglican church. The architecture symbolises the other links between our countries. In my own case, as a fellow of the British Computer Society, I was welcomed by the Secretary of the Indian equivalent, and we had the chance to exchange informally views on computing research and development. Highlighting the importance of the Commonwealth – similar links abound around the planet.

Bhaskar's view? If the Mugal Empire, which preceded the Brits, had continued, Gandhi would have been beheaded!

The key message from the assignment in our context is the vital necessity for appropriate institutions and legal frameworks which the Empire and Commonwealth created. We designed various IT features for Sika including for instance a communications network to their research department, their production factory, their marketing and sales outfits, and the selection of appropriate high-level development systems which could greatly improve their system's implementation, both in speed and reliability.[21] This

---

[21] SSADM Version 4 was then the most favoured system in the UK. I don't recommend readers to explore its unbelievable complexity unless they are feeling really fit! But having mastered it, it could be invaluable, bearing in mind the astonishing fragility being shown nowadays in most systems even by large corporations

was the area where I, funded by BESO, was brought in to add British expertise.

The picture is by Daniel, painting the Writer's Building circa 1790, a delightful contrast with the life and bustle of modern Kolkatta/Calcutta.

But Sika's foremost need was for a stock control system, of which there is a vast range of very sophisticated packages available in the UK. But because of India's lack of effective enforcement of copyright law, no standard off-the-peg software could be found. And when I returned to the UK, I found no software vendors who would touch the project with a bargepole. This despite detailed discussion meetings with eager Mancunian software houses. Views in the trade are that it's a one-sale situation – sell one copy and that's your lot – it'll be

---

and banks. As I write the UK's major bank, National Westminster, has been in grave difficulty servicing its customers for two days.

pirated all over everywhere, and you have no effective redress. Imagine the consequences – thousands of able Indian programmers all busily reinventing a well-known wheel which could be bought off the shelf in countries where copyright law was enforced. Great fun for the Bengali programmers – reinventing a package, as against tailoring an existing one, is challenging and enjoyable! Much better than tailoring and parameterising someone else's product. Another fundamental lesson from the assignment, which was tremendously rewarding – but voluntary – came from the two able young systems analysts with whom I worked. A bright pair of friends. When I first met them I asked them, as I did in most assignments: "What's the Bengali (or whatever) phrase for 'no problem'?"

I'd usually be told "Hakuna matata," (the Swahili) or whatever. "But why do you want to know?"

"Because whenever I hear hakuna matata, I know I have a real problem."

Corny perhaps, but it breaks the ice, you usually get a pleased guffaw, and people compete and hasten to grab you briefcase and assist you to the company car, etc. "Hakuna Matata Bwana or Sahib or Effendi or whatever!" and away it's snatched.

But in this case Renatu responded casually: "Ah, but here in Calcutta we have no problems. Only solutions!"

Before leaving I had a valedictory chat with them

"Suppose you guys will be completing this project in a year or so?" They looked at each other.

"Oh, no. In a year or less we'll be working in Australia." Perhaps I should have warned their boss, head of their software firm. Losing two key analysts halfway through would cause him grief. But I didn't. They'd become close friends. He was a pain in the neck!

*

Continuing the industrial theme, I can't resist showing the

cover below. Headrick writes to the ingenious theory that the development of technology in Europe was directed at empire. Rather like asserting that Microsoft's objectives in developing Windows were to dominate the Third World. In fact the motives, I think, were idealism, religion, exploration of the future, and having a lot of fun. Headrick instances the unscrupulous development of the steamboat and of medicinal drugs. In his view (my impression) a matter of battle, murder, and sudden plunder. We will see next how important these two were for civilisation and happiness in Kigezi.

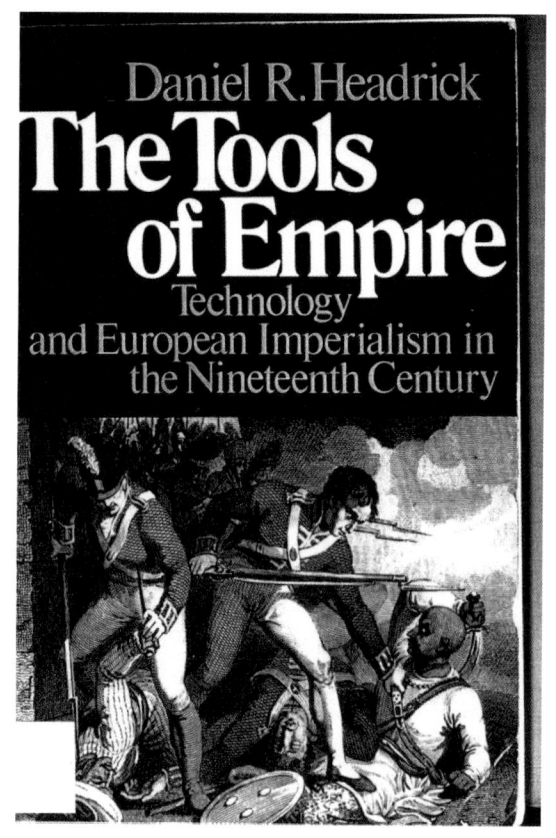

Graphic from Rhodes House, Oxford.

A Margaret Job

Not all initiatives in Commonwealth collaboration achieved their objectives.

Ferranti was a British electronics and computing giant in Manchester with a tremendous history of innovation since the 19th century.

After computers like Atlas and Orion, some of the earliest computers in the world, Ferranti had to select a successor. Following thorough research they decided the design and products from a Canadian firm were the best available, and after negotiations the Canadian machine was adopted, initially named Ferranti Packard, later renamed the 1900 Series.

It was a pleasing example of Commonwealth cooperation. Probably the foremost example in computing was the Canadians' lead in the invention of teletext, with some British involvement. These are the large multi-coloured text characters, 40 per line, seen on nearly all TV sets. Important also, I found on an assignment in Hungary, for enabling agricultural marketing after the fall of Communism. How, when you've abandoned top-down state pricing systems, do you set and promulgate produce prices in a market-driven economy? The answer was to use nationwide TV to display the various prices pertaining in different areas of the country at mid-day on weekdays.

Continuing in the vein of Commonwealth collaboration: with government pressure, one of the earliest great 1900 mainframes was allocated to Melbourne University in Australia. A recipe you might think for disaster – always keep your first customers on your doorstep so that you can sort out the inevitable glitches and take them to lunch. But it went ahead and when production and systems-testing of the massive water-cooled computer had been completed, they had to get it to the ship for Australia with an absolute minimum of vibration. The machine was on the third floor on the side of the works which overlooked the Peak Forest canal. The best solution seemed to the Production Supervisor to be to dangle the machine from special girders outside the walls and position a barge below it in the canal. Then spin the machine round to line up with the barge. Drop her down into it. Cruise down the canal to the docks. Dead flat water, no locks. Just like that. Not a problem.

The necessary crane, skids and derricks were set up, and the beast was dragged and slid into position. Lowering commenced, with some creaking and swaying. Watched by an anxious crowd on the far bank. After 3 feet down there was a sharp crack and a wire broke. The mainframe hurtled down into the barge and on through the bottom – they were heavy machines. The audience were appalled. The barge crew swam ashore. They were appalled. Everyone was appalled.

The then Managing Director or CEO was a choleric individual and it was known that male messengers bearing unwelcome tidings to him were usually shot. If not shot, then shot out of the company.

The CEO had a charming personal assistant, Margaret. This was clearly a Margaret job

The Production Supervisor briefed Margaret and went home for a fortnight's well-earned leave.[22]

---

[22] The computing industry has long had a succession of charismatic, assertive, and idiosyncratic managers – Ed Mack in ICL, TJ Watson in IBM, Steve Jobs in Apple, and numerous others. I like the tale of the Chief Executive of a Midwest manufacturer. He took great pride in knowing all his large staff by name. He was taking a couple of key customers round the production floor one morning, remembered the name of one worker, Patrick O'Reilly, and addressed him:
"Hallo, Patrick," he said. "How's the wife?"
A reasonable enquiry to make, he thought – most Irishmen have wives.
Patrick replied: "Oh thanks, Sorr. Still dead, Sorr."

Graphic from author.

Chapter 6

Religion, Health, and Medicine

(Strange perhaps to link these three topics together, but they are often closely intertwined.)

Soon after we arrived in Kabale we were invited out to see the Sharps. Their story indicates the role of the Christian missions, in this case the protestant Anglican CMS (Church Missionary Society) at its best.

I described Lake Bunyonyi, the Lake of the little birds in Chapter 1. In the junction of its three arms were two islands, one about 2 miles long and 200 feet high, the other a small triangle a quarter of a mile long. These islands, at the time when the Brits came, were the centre of a growing witch cult which was gradually dominating South West Uganda, in competition with the rule of kings like the Kabaka of Uganda.

The cult practices were as savage and vicious as were recently the allied practices of kidoni in the eastern Congo, and Uganda, the LRA – Lords Resistance Army, and to a degree of the Kenyan Mau Mau.

The Brits decided to counter this movement, and to do so they portaged a steel boat piecemeal the hundred and twenty miles of trough track from Lake Victoria. They then assembled it and attacked and overthrew the cult leaders on the bigger of the two islands. Then as a token of the potential of Christianity, Dr and Mrs Sharp were invited in from the CMS in the UK. There were no roads in those days, so they came in 1921 on a 1915 model Triumph motorcycle (with the long up-swept handlebars and clanking cantilevered forks of those times) all the way up the thousand-and-odd miles from the sea at Mombasa. They built a hut on the bigger island and established a small hospital and a church and patient quarters in a model village. Since leprosy then was endemic in this region, they called the island Leper Island and soon had large numbers of lepers coming from great distances around. Leprosy is a fairly contagious and immensely disfiguring bacterial disease of the nerves, affecting the eyes, skin, and limbs, sometimes involving hands and sometimes causing fingers to be shortened as cartilage is absorbed into the body. The normal indigenous practice in Kigezi, whereby families took care of their sick people, did not apply in this case. People were filled with horror, much as in the case of the leper cured by Christ in the Gospel according to St Luke 5 vv12-16. Leprosy would not be fully curable for another sixty years. The leper colony grew fast and was immensely successful. As it developed the Sharps built for themselves a cottage on the small island and laid it out very beautifully. That was and is known as Sharps Island.

We were told to arrive at 3pm, having been warned by our friends that the Sharps, who were members of the CMS Rwanda mission, worked to Rwandan time. Their three o'clock was our four o'clock. We were allowed (this once) to use the government launch. We drove over the hilltop and down to Chabahinga where the boat was waiting, and enjoyed a voyage two miles round Leper Island and to Sharps Island. There they met us. The island by this time looked extraordinarily beautiful. From the north it widened out in a triangle, and had been landscaped and treescaped to match, with three yews planted at 10-year intervals. The sprawling house was made of sun-dried brick, and the roof of tiles manufactured at the local Catholic mission, using a technology from Cognac in France. The interior was similar to those you find in splendid old settlers' houses in Zambia or Zimbabwe, with parquet tiled floors made from the local hardwood known as muvule. The two great missionaries were in their late 60s, still warm and friendly, and Dr Sharp still indulged his perhaps unchristian love of big game shooting. Tables were made from elephants' ears and ash trays from elephants' feet. Buck trophies of various breeds were up on the walls. We had a pleasant tea with them, and I sensed, as I did with other missionaries, that their relationship with the Protectorate Administration involved certain tensions. Particularly so in Kigezi since the political allegiances centred, as in Belfast, or Liverpool and Glasgow, between the Protestants and Catholics.

That description of the Sharps and their island and the general achievement of the Sharps introduces the process of creating healthcare in Kigezi. By the time I arrived there in 1958 there was a well-established health service with Health Assistants distributed among the counties, and three hospitals in the district.

A description of a typical district officer's safari was given in Chapter 4, and through these safaris, but most of all through pressure from the District Council, the Chiefs and medical orderlies, facilities for basic hygiene, particularly of course for pit latrines, existed throughout the district. Poorly built latrines are a serious source of health risks due to flies laying their eggs on the faeces and causing serious diseases like hepatitis A or E-coli. No latrines are of course even more of a threat to health.

Repeating a key story, I was to join my daughter 20 years later in Hoima where she was working to introduce rural water supplies and AIDS prevention. It's worth repeating, because it's so fundamental to health services: We went to a very big baraza being run by the District Health Officer, with about 300 people attending. He exhorted the people on the question of hygiene:

"When the British were here 80% of you had latrines. Truly now only 20%. Tell me why. Why were you building the latrines? Was it for the British?"

He got a good laugh. But it indicates the effectiveness of the early administration.

Over the recent fifty years, BESO, British Executive Service Overseas, was a general source of volunteer experts for technical improvement in many developing countries in the Commonwealth. Brits, for example, who had reached senior levels in their professions and welcomed the chance to put their experience to good effect in developing countries. Designers in the Potteries, for example, had long experience in the design and manufacture of toilets – Shanks being a well-known variety. A friend, Donald Beach, made several trips for BESO and to great effect. The construction of these vital features of civilised living is complicated and demanding.

Tony Benn wrote as we saw that he did not "believe that this was motivated by Christian charity or designed to help the poor benighted natives." If so, and setting aside the pejorative phrase "poor benighted natives", what was it motivated by? The volunteers were unpaid do-gooders. They would hate the description. But that's what they were.

Chapter 7

Historical Background to the Uganda Protectorate

I hope readers now have a general feel for the background, so I'll fill in on some history. The original formation of Uganda Protectorate in 1894 resulted from three main factors. The first was a letter and articles written by HM Stanley about his astonishing and brutal travels through Africa from Livingstone's church near Lake Tanganyika, northwards to Uganda and Lake Victoria and then westwards to the mouth of the Congo River. Right through the African heart of darkness, as it was movingly described. His account particularly singled out his time at the court of the Kabaka in Buganda and the atrocities that he witnessed. He urged the Brits – especially readers of the *Daily Telegraph* – to bring civilisation to the area and to enter into missionary activity. This received immense support in Victorian England because people believed they had a duty to bring Christian civilisation to the area. Which, I think, despite Tony Benn's view, is just what they did.

Secondly, pressure from the commercials, led by Alexander McKinnon of McKenzie based in Zanzibar who wanted to open up the centre of the continent to trade.

Thirdly, the accounts by Speke, Burton, and Stanley of the evils of the slave trade between that area and Arabia. In some ways this was even worse than the slave trade across the Atlantic by the British – for example very many of the young males, who were chained together in the lines of slaves being taken North to the Gulf states, were destined to be castrated as eunuchs at the courts of the sultans. And as I saw in the war zone of the Sudan in 1993, persists to this day.[23] *The Observer* described in a full-page article, the traffic in slaves to the Gulf only fifteen years ago.

This overrode the Gladstone government's wish to avoid any further African entanglements, most of which were recognised to bring costly implications. Eventually, as the Cabinet minutes record, popular pressure and the missionaries pushed the government into creating the Uganda Protectorate. The grounds given by the government were that they were concerned to protect the Nile waters for Egypt. At that time the Nile was virtually impassable to the north as a result of a massive swamp area called the Sudd of 30,000 km sq., and further swamp areas in the part of Uganda now known as Lake Kyoga. Any attempt to control the Nile at that stage in history would have been both ludicrous and impossible. Even now it would present massive engineering problems, although as the world emphasis on water intensifies it may be reopened. This is relevant to the general debate on the notorious – and arguable – "Scramble for Africa" which is discussed in Chapter 12. Its misconceptions as well as its iniquities. How about a "What if" approach as is commonly used in 21st-century industry. What if the Europeans hadn't scrambled?

---

[23] This was a World Bank assignment known as SKADP for the Setup of the Control and Monitoring and Evaluation system for Integrated Rural Development Project in Southern Kordofan, including design, training and management, involving staff from five different ministries.

Ugandan Independence

In our first two years the general affection for the Brits surprised and pleased me. People commonly waved to you from their holdings as you drove past. I recall particularly a Saza chief of immense distinction warmly shaking the hand of Gerard Barnes at the end of his final safari.

"Webale okututegyeka ssebo."[24]

"Thank you for teaching us," said with heartfelt sincerity.

But then the impact of the transistor radio and the LSE (London School of Economics) attacked the easy relationship. Transistor radios became commonplace, and through them was beamed all manner of anti-colonial propaganda, from the Second World, i.e. the Communist USSR, the Russian Empire, and from many sources indigenous to Africa.

Why do I single out the LSE? Slightly humorously. But Hugh Fraser, the DC Kigezi, received a letter from the Colonial Office, then under Labour control, advocating that we send a senior chief to the LSE for training in administration. The prospectus looked good, and no expenditure by the elected Local Government Council was involved. So he selected one of the most promising younger saza chiefs, let's call him Fred. Fred was naturally delighted, and went to the LSE for three months.[25] On his return from

---

[24] This is a nice example of the fascinating and sophisticated grammar of nearly all Bantu languages, as we'll explore later. *Oku* – the infinitive of the verb; *tu* – us; *tegya* – teach; *tegyeka* – cause to be taught. How did this wonderful intellectual structure evolve over most of the continent?

[25] Later in life I had several opportunities to lecture and discuss at the LSE key innovative ideas like the use of computing to help support agricultural development among smallholder farmers, or the provision of credit. LSE is a vital, forward-looking institution,

LSE Fred had become immensely hostile. Gone was the ready smile and rapport. Gone was Fred's vigorous forward-looking leadership, and it took six months to get him back on track.

I introduced to you earlier to the Sharps, universally revered by the Bakiga for a life spent serving them and creating two hospitals and helping with countless dispensaries. But at this stage, in 1960, an ageing Mrs Sharp wandered as was her wont around the 'market' – really an open field with produce on wooden stalls or blankets. A big tribesman came up to her, looked into her eyes and spat in her face. None of the bystanders demurred. It shocked us.

Our rapport with the chiefs was less easy, becoming slightly cagey.

So views from distinguished people like the Katikiro of Bunyoro, and Alan Forward, ADC to the Governor, that the Brits left far too early, are, I think, wrong. We could not have stayed on without facing an uprising which might have undone much of what had been achieved. Occasionally I think that perhaps we should have done so, acting as the anvil on which a young nation might have been forged. Nationalism, they taught us at Oxford, was based on "myths of the past and dreams of the future". And if you build on myths which are just concoctions, you're building your nation on sand. But, judging from the tragic histories of the ex-Belgian colonies, which plunged into chaos, I doubt that we left too

---

but with an impatient bias against conventional wisdom and the heritage of the past. They had a formidable lift, dubbed the "Pater Noster", i.e. Our Father, the Lord's Prayer, because you supposedly prayed, and prayed devoutly, before entering it. It was a continuously rotating serial belt of cabinets seven feet by four by three. You stepped in one as it passed, were whisked up or down, and stepped out hastily as you reached your destination. I was tempted to see what happened if you stayed on board as it reached the top and came over and down again – would you emerge standing on your head or your feet?

early. And were we capable of policing many peoples all round the globe against their will? We were recruited to the Uganda Government in '57 and told to expect a career of perhaps ten or fifteen years, because the people in the Colonial Office and at the centre of the Uganda government, in Entebbe, well realised where we were. That we were about to take off on the down-face of a gathering wave which, in the climate of the times, was unstoppable. Just like a physical wave approaching a shelving shore; it rolls gently on indefinitely, until it reaches the coast and the critical shallows when its height is the same as the depth to the bottom. Then the lower half of the wave drags on the sea bed, the top starts to overtake and curl over, and suddenly it breaks and crashes on the beach. That was Uganda. Once you had democratically elected politicians there was no way they would tolerate government by an unelected group of foreigners, particularly foreigners of the wrong skin colour. Self-respect demanded freedom.

We want independence, they said. Independence, willy-nilly. None of your American constitutional nonsense. We want full independence on the Westminster model. And we want it now.

Chapter 8

Entomology – the Study of Insects

    I would like to introduce a burly genial fellow who became a great friend. Curly brown hair kept fairly long, English-looking though actually a Scot, humorous, sometimes caustic towards officialdom. His name is Angus McCrae and he was a Ugandan government entomologist, attacking insect-borne and parasite-borne diseases. He worked at first mostly with the WHO (UN World Health Organisation) malaria eradication project in Kigezi.

Graphic from Sainsbury collection, British museum.

But I got to know him well drinking through the night a bottle of Johnny Walker Black Label whisky with his girlfriend in his house in Kampala. We were trying to measure the rate of growth of a creeper as we were chatting and supping. My wife Alison was busy having our first daughter, Diana, in Nakasero Hospital close by. We had been given two days' leave for the event, as was usual. Imagine the worry – having to get the dates right, then driving 250 miles on potholed unsurfaced roads to the capital, hoping that labour would not start en route, but would start when you arrived. After the two days I would have to leave Alison and drive 250 miles back and resume duty on the Congo border. The general practice for expats' childbirth was for the husband to drive the expectant mother fast along the bumpy, very rough track from Kampala out to the Veterinary Research farm. The bumps and rolling might, if you were lucky, succeed in inducing labour. For us it had succeeded. Diana was born and the creeper had grown five inches.

Angus related how his boss, Fred, came to be appointed Head of Entomology, Uganda Protectorate Administration. A key role, concerned with the many insects, etc. (dudus, Angus called them affectionately) which caused diseases like malaria or onchocerciasis. Fred, the boss, had left university in 1938 with a degree in biology. He decided to apply to join the Colonial Service, where biologists were greatly needed. In due course he was invited for interview (as were we all) in the august headquarters of the Colonial Service, Church House, Westminster. He entered a vast, oblong, panelled room, stern portraits of formidable people on the walls, a long mahogany table at the far end, at which sat five men. Their backgrounds were unexplained, but rumour had it that there was a psychologist at the left-hand end and a minister of religion at the right. They started to quiz him. The man in the centre, big and choleric with bulging eyes, was continually deferred to. He interrupted Fred's answer to one question:

"Do you play goff, Entwhistle?"

"No, sir."

And a few minutes later, another interruption:

"Do you play bridge, Entwhistle?"

"No, sir."

"Not much of a grace to the social life of a station. What?"

"Well, I'd try my best, sir."

That virtually finished the interview, and in due course a rejection came, and Fred joined a consultancy.

He did well in the war, finishing as a distinguished full colonel. He reapplied to join the Colonial Service in response to an advert for an entomologist, and found himself again in Church House, Westminster. But this time in a comfortable office, talking to a single civil servant.

"Do come in, very glad to see you, colonel."

"Do have some coffee, colonel."

"Do you like ginger nuts, Colonel? I'm very partial to them."

The civil servant's knowledge of entomology seemed limited to the fact that it concerned insects, but he was immensely friendly and deferential. The fact that Fred actually wasn't an entomologist didn't matter too much.

"Don't worry," he said, "you'll soon pick it all up."

So Fred was accepted, and went out to Uganda, and picked it all up, and made his reputation as a world expert. Not a bad system for handling the unknown.

*

In his time in Kigezi, Angus worked with Dr De Zuluetta of WHO, the World Health Organisation. They targeted on the complete eradication of malaria in the entire district, no less. And in fact, if their technique had been applied simultaneously throughout the malarial areas of the world, the disease might have disappeared from the face of the earth.

The operation involved was immense. The objective was to break the cycle of the parasite's life (plasmodium falciparum), which involves hosting in the female Anopheles malaria mosquito larva, where it grows in still water. Then it hatches. The adult mosquito eventually roams to get a fill of blood from a human host, and in doing so passes the parasite on to the human, where it lodges in the liver and spreads in the red blood cells throughout the body, causing violent bouts of sweating and fever about every 48 hours. Debilitating, often death-dealing.

So all houses throughout the district were sprayed by teams with knapsack sprayers containing insecticide (DDT I think) to kill the mosquitoes. And all the population were treated with antimalarial drugs. Amazingly the project succeeded. But the migrant nature of much employment in Kigezi – young men to the copper mines as described in Chapter 19 – meant that the parasite was eventually carried back to the district by returning labourers. In fact, in 1969, the WHO formally abandoned this approach to eradication. Now, 40 years later, the idea of eradication on a global scale is gaining momentum. But the problems especially in Africa are thought by many to be insurmountable.[19] Think of the chaotic nature of the Congo as described in Butcher's *Blood River* to realise how acute are the problems in the worst cases.

Angus related how they were halted on one trip by a herd of elephants which straddled a ford and blocked their way. They pressed the truck's hooter, but the elephants paid not a blind bit of attention. A Mutwa pigmy watched with interest, skin-clad and stinking. Angus remembered that the Batwa pigmies from the forests and mountains were said to have a close affinity with the animal world. He discussed this with Bitakuri, the driver. They agreed to try offering the Mutwa ten shillings if he could shift the elephants, and so they did. The pigmy turned confidently towards the herd and harangued them in the typical Mutwa voice, a sort of strangulated high-pitched squeal with a curious bass undertone.

"What's he saying?" asked Angus.

"He say, 'Elephants bugger off.'"

But they didn't. Not a blind bit of attention.

The Mutwa was frantic to get the ten shillings. He picked up a large handful of stones, ran towards the lead male and hurled them at him. The elephant shuffled and swung his trunk peevishly, then led his followers away. The truck crossed the ford and continued along the track.

Onchocerciasis

This disease, also known as a river blindness, was common in Uganda along the rivers. It is caused by infection by a roundworm from the black fly Mbwa fly, whose larva spread throughout the body. When they die their symbionts cause the host system, i.e. the humans, to release immune responses which can destroy tissue in the eyes. The disease is confined to primates – men and monkeys – and an estimated 240,000 cases of blindness occurred recently, mostly in sub-Saharan Africa and South America.

Studying this disease and how to cure it was one of Angus' major targets. I don't know the detail of what he did, but I do recall a splendid account of how he borrowed the tiny police Cessna monoplane, and cavorted down the winding Semliki River, bombing it with DDT to try to kill off the black fly. An early attempt to control it which I guess would nowadays raise horrified protests. Drugs are now available, generally named ivermectin. These have to be taken once every six months over a three years. Why, in that case, are there 270,000 cases of blindness in 2000?

A very successful control programme involving Angus'

idea – bombing the fast-flowing rivers – was launched in 1974, covering 30 million – yes, 30 million – people.

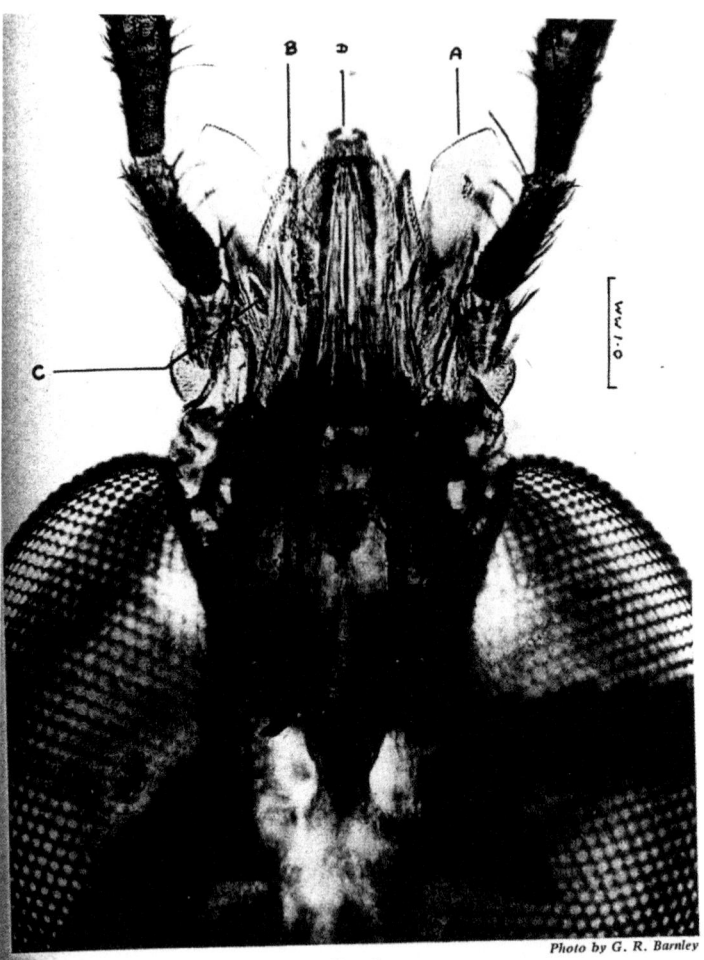

Photo by G. R. Barnley

FIG. 2

Biting mouth parts of *Simulium damnosum*. The labium or 'tongue' has been removed in order to display the saw-edged mandible (A) and the file-toothed maxillae (B). The mandibles are in life hinged together like the blades of a pair of scissors but they have been disarticulated and displaced laterally from beneath the labrum-epiphyrynx (D). The 'hinge', a chitinous knob, can be seen at (C).

Graphics from Rhodes House, Oxford.

Angus had a distinguished career over 40 years, despite his divorce and a seriously handicapped son. He died in 2000, halfway through writing what was intended to be a definitive work on the Emperor Moth for Oxford University.

> the Mbwa Fly works with two pairs of cutting organs; the mandibles, which are hinged exactly like a pair of scissors and have serrated blades like dressmakers' pinking shears; and the maxillae which are pointed organs edged with teeth very similar to those of a carpenter's rasp. By a combination of the processes of snipping and filing the fly excavates a hole in the skin and tears a superficial capillary blood-vessel. The drop of blood is then sucked up 'haustorially' by a disk-shaped tongue somewhat similar to that of the common house-fly.
>
> The process of scraping the wound is one which invokes every mechanism the skin possesses for preventing bleeding by causing the blood to clot and seal the hole. As the tongue cannot suck up solid material the fly has had to elaborate a special technique for preventing the clotting of blood. All blood-sucking insects are equipped with salivary glands which secrete anti-coagulant enzymes and it is this material which causes the irritation almost invariably associated with an insect bite. The Mbwa Fly, moreover, has very large salivary glands and has developed the whole of its proventriculus (fore-gut or crop) as an organ for the storage of salivary secretion. When it bites it has the very nasty habit of vomiting into the wound a volume of saliva about equal to that of the drop of blood. It puddles the saliva about in the wound with its tongue and then sucks up the mixture. This vomiting of saliva and the working of it into the wound is of course an ideal method of transmitting parasites from host to vector and from vector to host. Furthermore, the saliva also contains a hormone that acts as a tropic agent, concentrating the larval skin forms of the parasitic worm *Onchocerca volvulus* to the site of the bite so that they are sucked up with the blood.
>
> This biting method, involving the release by the skin of considerable quantities of histamine and the application of a large drop of saliva containing anti-coagulant and tropic enzymes produces the painful weal with an inflamed centre characteristic of the Mbwa bite. The bite is so irritating that to refrain from scratching is almost impossible and infective dirt is frequently rubbed into the wound and local ulcers result.
>
> The life history of the Simuliidae is unusual and interesting. The female fly is fertilized by waiting males immediately on emergence from the pupa and after it has had a blood meal it retires to a damp and shaded environment where its ovaries mature. In about 96 hours the fly is ripe and makes for a suitable breeding site. In the case of *S. damnosum*, the choice of site is limited to violently agitated water where the concentration of dissolved or suspended oxygen is at a maximum. The many falls and rapids on the Victoria Nile provide the ideal conditions. The female settles on vegetation trailing into the water or on an exposed rock and deposits some 250 eggs at the water edge. The eggs hatch within a period of between a few hours and a day, and the first stage larvae then emerge. This emergence is one of the critical periods in the life cycles: unless the larva can attach itself to some under-water support it will be swept away and perish. To this end the larva is equipped with silk glands in the head with which it spins a 'life-line'.

Description from Uganda Journal, Rhodes House.

Bilharzia or Schistosomiasis

Bilharzia is a vicious disease which attacks millions of people who live near the water in the tropics. It is also known as schistosomiasis. The parasite eggs hatch in the faeces of infected humans and enter into the feet of freshwater snails. The life cycle routes from the fresh water snail, where the miracidia hatch on contact with the water and emerge as free-swimming parasites. They lodge on the human skin and after two days penetrate it and swim up the veins into the lungs. Thence they develop and travel to the brain and to the liver. They cause five different effects of the disease and are usually severely damaging, and chronic but not usually lethal. Though sometimes they cause bowel cancer and death. In my time in Uganda there was only one possible cure and that was to insert a syringe into the stomach of the sufferer and to pump in – very painful – sufficient poison (antimony, I think) to kill off the flukes but not quite kill the sufferer. He or she usually looked grey and unwell for many months before recovering.

Graphic from sainsbury collection, British Museum.

It hit most people who worked near the water, and most of my colleagues in Fisheries Department. As a keen sailor, I often envied John Stoneman, local fisheries officer, for his splendid job cruising between the fishing villages on Lake Albert, where the great film *African Queen* was made. For our leisure pursuits we used to sail our dinghy well off-shore and only swim when there was sufficient of a lop to be sure that the hippos and crocodiles and flukes would say inshore.

So, to summarise, the problem of bilharzia occurs when a person is wading in shallow water. The flukes are circulating, seeking a target. They find the leg, penetrate, and swim up the veins until they reach the liver. There are they lodge and breed. Once a month the activity greatly increases, and severe illness results.

Let's contrast this with the situation when I was working in the Sudan in the 1990s. I was returned invalided out to the UK as described earlier and one of the problems they found was bilharzia. How I had contracted it was very strange because there was no standing water in the desert areas of around Khartoum and no rivers near us in the far side of the Sahara in Kadugli. It can last up to twenty years, so perhaps I had picked it up in Uganda. I sometimes noticed a monthly spell of lassitude and unease – possibly the parasite's life cycle. Anyway I was taken into the Liverpool hospital for tropical diseases. The doctor asked me to lay face down naked on a stretcher. He then proceeded to glove up and finger around inside my anus. I said to him, "Are you sure this is necessary?"

He was extremely annoyed, and said, "Yes indeed." After a couple of hours he got the results and told me that I had in fact contracted bilharzias. He gave me 24 pills which had to be taken before sleeping.

Next morning the results were completely clear. It's an astonishing example of the way in which modern research and medicine has benefited humanity in the last half century.

The above is an oversimplification. Quite how astonishing this achievement is can only be understood if you read the piece in Wikipedia and try to grasp the fascinating complexity of the parasite's life cycle and wonder how on earth it was unravelled. That was what entomologists like Angus McCrae were all about. Jeremy Paxman ignores the diseases in his index. Richard Gott writes of the "great plagues of empire" He makes no mention of the fact that the Empire and Commonwealth were the great organisations which helped to fight them for all mankind. Not a message he relishes.[26]

Fisheries

Fisheries link surprisingly to entomology in this account.

Peter Holness was the Fisheries officer whom we met when he was a deputy returning officer and demanding the imprisonment of the local candidate in the 1958 election. He was a heavy, ruddy-complexioned Zimbabwean white who had been a tractor driver, and his choice may seem incongruous. However, by personality and manner he fitted his task well and got a great deal done in a very short time.

The policy was to use the swamps which characterised most smaller valleys in Kigezi as sources of protein. This would be done by digging out large fishponds about 30m by 20m to a depth of one and a half metres. One of the streams feeding the swamp would be diverted into this hole, and when the pond filled up, a fish called tilapia would be fed in. How they survived in the oxygen-deficient waters I don't know, but they did. Tilapia, or ngege, are fine, white-fleshed, and delicious, about the size of a small sea bass. Sufficient funds were supplied for local labour to dig the ponds out, and swiftly the district acquired these attractive and nutritious

---

[26] Britain's Empire" page 2, Richard Gott, Scandbook AB Sweden 2011

additions. I remember visiting my first pond on tour, and being shown by the gombolola chief, with great pride, the tilapia rising and thrashing around like trout in an English trout farm when grass was thrown in to feed them. I asked what was happening to the fish, and the answer was, "Oh, we don't eat them, because we are of the fish clan."

A splendid theme for those who wish to deride the colonial system. How did we get to encourage fishpond creation by people for whom fish was taboo? However, I probed further. In fact the fish were being caught, gutted, and sun-dried, and sold in markets to those of other clans to whom fish were not taboo. So the operation had been immensely successful.

One day in 1960, Angus McCrae joined a meeting with Dr de Zuluetta, the WHO head of the malaria eradication campaign and Holness, who had been called in, in the hotel conference room. The venue is significant. De Zuluetta had decided to avoid meeting in government offices. Angus sensed tension, and Holness appeared worried and mystified. Insects were not his patch. De Zuluetta rapidly and forcefully attacked the whole fishing farm concept and execution. The ponds, he insisted, were harbouring mosquito larvae, and would totally destroy the UN's malaria eradication operation. Peter Holness protested vigorously, but he was inarticulate and unable to counteract the man's view, and of course the logic. As a result the fishpond project was abandoned, the ponds were drained, and Holness was left to run the relatively insignificant fisheries on Lake George. He swiftly resigned.

Referring back to the critics: **"The one time Empire builders were reduced to the status of clerks, buried deeper and deeper under mountains of paper and red tape."**

Was Angus McCrae being twitched at the end of a cable from the clerks in the UK? Were any of us? I suggest not.

Chapter 9

Agricultural Research

There is a saying in the UN's Food and Agriculture Organisation's HQ in Rome which reads, if I remember rightly:

"There can be no greater achievement than to make two stalks of grass to grow where only one grew before." The picture shows the basics which we'll discuss below.

We came across John Purseglove – "Bwana Fertility" – in Chapter 1. I'd like now to explore what he and other research scientists did by looking at his later career. His description on the Dutch herbarium website shows an astonishing set of achievements. Quite a guy. It's significant that it is a Dutch, not a British website, that he is little known in the UK until a recent biography, and that the great research institute at East Malling where he served is a shadow of its former self, resulting from short termism in the 1980s and since. Short termism which also hit the great Australian CSIRO's (Commonwealth Scientific and Industrial Research Organisation) agricultural activities. Though their scope is still fascinating. I'll follow the Dutch document on Purseglove with a description of typical procedures involved in agricultural research worldwide including those we saw in the Yemen, and in the great range of international research institutes like IRRI (the International Rice Research Institute), and in Malaysia the RRI (Rubber Research Institute),. We will finally cover the research at East Malling, directed solely at fruit research, particularly their work screening apple rootstocks which changed the way apple trees are grown around the world. The dwarfing rootstock M9 changed the size of apple trees, dramatically affecting ease of harvesting for example. I remember harvesting apples as a student in a Kentish orchard, precarious up your ladder, high in a twenty foot tree. No need nowadays to leave the ground.

Figure 1. Dissected "pin" and "thrum" flowers of *Primula vulgaris* showing relative positions of the sexual flower parts: stamen, stigma, style, and ovary.

A Great Agricultural Research Scientist

Purseglove, John William

From the Dutch herbarium website:
www.nationaalherbarium.nl/fmcollectors/p/PursegloveJW/htm

Born: 1912, Derbyshire, UK.

Career:

Was educated at Manchester University (B.Sc., honours in Botany, 1934), at Gonville & Caius College, Cambridge University (1934-1935), and the Imp. College of Tropical Agriculture in Trinidad (1935-36). Agricultural Officer in Uganda, 1936-52; seconded from the Colonial Agricultural Service as Lecturer in Tropical Agriculture, Cambridge University, 1952-54; in 1954 appointed Director, Botanic Gardens, Singapore.

He resigned in 1957, and was appointed Professor of Botany at the Imp. College of Trinidad. About 1967 appointed Advisor on Tropical Crops for the Ministry of Overseas Development, working at East Malling Research Station, Maidstone, Kent, England.

He travelled extensively in Africa south of the Sahara.

Durio purseglovei Kosterm was named after him.

Collecting Localities

Malay Peninsula. From **1954** *onwards.* A little in *Singapore*, Port Dickson, *etc.*-**1955**. Fraser's Hill (Apr. 15-25, P4092-4338). *NW. Borneo*, *Sarawak*: Kuching (Sept. 12), Ham Kitang (13), peat swamp forest at Setapok (14), Karenga sand, Mile 6 Penrissen Road (14), Semnagoh Forest Reserve (14), Bau (15), Sebanding Swamp Forest, Lundu (18), Gunung Gading,

Lundu 100-1000 ft. (19), Lundu (20), Sematan (21), Kp. Pueh (21), G. Pueh (22), Kp. Pueh (25), Sematan (27), Kuching (29).-**1956**. *NW. Borneo, Sarawak* (May 15-June 13): in Bako National Park, Sungei Tau, Sungei Miyang Bukit Mersing and Tatau. *Malay Peninsula*: Mersing, G. Pulai in Johore; Fraser's Hill.-**1957**. *Sarawak*: Bako National Park (Feb. 2-18) with Moh. Shah bin Haji Moh. Nur.

Collections

Herb. Sing. [SING]; dupl. at Kew [K], Leiden [L], Sarawak Mus. Herb. [SAR] (Borneo specim.), and the Arn. Arb. [A]. In Sarawak (1955) assisted by Moh. Shah bin_Haji_Moh. Nur (see there) and from time to time by members of the Museum and Forest Department Staff, Sarawak, collecting nos P4351-P4856, numbered in his own series; in 1956 nos P4877-5490 (Sarawak), etc.

P Nos to be cited under his full name.

Malaysian collections begin at P4001 (series begun in Uganda). Uganda collections in Kawanda Herb. And E. Afr. Herb., Nairobi.

Dupl. of Gesneriaceae to Herb. Edinb. [E], of Ficus spp. to Mr Corner (Cambridge [CGE]), and Sterculiaspp to Mr Kostermans (Bogor [BO]).

What is agricultural research all about?

Let's look at the activities carried out typically at East Malling, which was John Purseglove's final posting.

Graphic from author's photo.

The institute's objective is to develop new varieties of fruits notably apples and strawberries, and they have been immensely successful in doing so. The apples usually are grafted onto rootstock, the ground-based tree which has been selected for its reliability and robustness. The most famous rootstock developed by East Malling became virtually standard worldwide, was distributed free (unlike the French Golden Delicious which was based on it), and is named M9. To take an Oriental example, the Malaysian Rubber Research Institute (RRI) has developed a rootstock for rubber, and the latest derivative when I was there was named RRI 603. In using it, a diagonal cut was sliced through the rootstock and then the selected rubber tree was tied on to match it. The Malaysians have tried adding yet a further item for the top of the desired tree, i.e. the canopy. A three part tree.

At East Malling, they go to the flower of the tree in question, then take a tiny brush to the anther at the top of the stamen, the spike in the flower's centre, and take the pollen, rather like a bee or other fertilising insect. Then they take that pollen on the brush to a target flower on another tree and place it at the stamen's base. This fertilised flower then produces a new apple, as shown in the picture. The blue ribbons and white ribbons carry identification information for that particular tree for data handling, e.g. statistical analysis using standard deviations.

Graphic from author's photo.

This cross fertilisation is done for a number of possible cultivars, and the progress and performance of the new cultivars are carefully monitored.

This is a simplification of a number of painstaking procedures for example DNA testing. Or testing the new apple's resistance to insect attack. The triple-glazed greenhouses in the picture are sealed, and insects are put in. Then after a given time in this controlled environment the number of surviving insects are counted.

Graphic from author's photo.

Similar procedures are carried out on many plants – we covered the activities on rice varieties when discussing research in the Yemen. The Commonwealth dimension is very significant – one of the East Malling team is currently with a research centre in the Eastern Cape in South Africa.

This research of course only covers the generation of new varieties against all manner of criteria, such as disease resistance or drought resistance or day length. In Colin Leakey's research in Uganda and the Philippines for example, they tested against kidding the poor plant – vanilla – that the day length was halved or whatever by closing and opening the greenhouse shutters to simulate night. The new industry, growing and marketing vanilla beans in Western Uganda was shown recently on TV. None of them were aware of Colin's work at Makerere University in Uganda forty years earlier on which their beans were probably derived.

Frank Cope, Research Director at Fisons, watched an experiment at East Malling to see if an automatically controlled system for the greenhouse ventilators was as good as the human gardeners. He overheard:

"What's the auto doing now, Fred?"

"It's closing down."

"Then we'll close down, Fred."

"Right."

Here, as in the Yemen with the short stem rice, unexpected characteristics can foul things up!

The research has to be followed by careful replication to produce numerous copies, and by the whole complicated process of getting these varieties established as we discussed for rubber with the Rubber Industry Smallholders Development Authority in Malaysia.

Agricultural Research Conclusion

In the nineteen fifties an appallingly Malthusian future was forecast by the UN for India and China and the Third world. Famines which would dwarf those in the past. The prognostications were of Malthusian disaster – deaths in millions as the population, growing explosively, swiftly outstripped the means of production.

It didn't happen. That it didn't happen was largely the achievement of the Green Revolution (research including new varieties of key crops, new approaches to cultivation, new types of fertiliser, pesticide and fungicides and so on), much of which was nurtured in research centres all over the Commonwealth. Much of it was spawned by the ARC Rothamsted and its 13 subordinates like East Malling, and by parallel activities e.g. by CSIRO in Australia.

The world now faces a similar scenario as a result of climate change and population explosion. Will our response this time match our response in the past?

Chapter 10

Agricultural Extension

All disciplines have jargon which is often obscure and annoying to the lay world. "Extension" in agriculture is the jargon word applied to the process of promulgating and advising on techniques of farming among the farming population by agricultural specialists. For First-World farming, extensionists are essentially consultants with individual contacts with individual farms. Our next-door farm for example is a dairy farm, and the government or private sector extensionist visits perhaps once monthly. He discusses the herd's performance, milk yields – butter fat content, antibiotics used – calving strategy, physical health. Then the milking technology, herringbone parlour layout. Then the pasture, the allocation of the fields to grazing in sequence, the growth rate of the grass (with a fascinating gadget that sits at the bottom of a walking stick). So the extensionist has a crucial advisory role.

But in Third-World agriculture the extensionists' tasks are even more central. And their activities were widely debated, refined. They affected all countries across the Commonwealth. The farmers – usually many thousands (300,000 in Malaysia's smallholder rubber sector) – are often untrained in new technologies. Sometimes they are over-eager to accept guidance from ill-qualified extensionists which can prove disastrous, sometimes so under-eager that techniques with immense potential have to be shelved. To illustrate the extensionists' importance, as we saw when describing agricultural research, the general consensus in the 1940s and

'50s was that countries like India and China were doomed in the immediate future to the chaotic implosion first forecast by the Cambridge economist, Thomas Malthus (pronounced malt house, they taught us in Cambridge) in the 1820s. Their populations would grow so much faster than the land's capability to support them that famine would rage, and pestilence would then deplete the weakened survivors, and civil governance would collapse. According to Malthus, war and disease were necessary to keep the population numbers in bounds, and to fight against this nemesis would only create even greater hardship and unhappiness for humanity. That collapse seemed in the 1950s to be inevitable in those countries which were heavily populated. But it never happened.

Agricultural research, led by institutions like the ARC in Rothamsted, and co-ordinated by the UN's FAO (Food and Agricultural Organisation) determined to fight this Malthusian process, and set up an immense range of carefully researched projects. We'll look at a few later to see how they worked, but the key conclusion for the present is that the appalling and inevitable disasters never actually happened. What prevented them was "The Green Revolution", a great range of experiments on staple crops like rice, maize, wheat, sorghum, finger millet and so on. For example to breed selectively new rice plants, new cultivars, which had shorter stalks[27] so that more of the nutrients in the soil could be available for increasing the nutrients in the grains for harvesting. Less stalk, more rice.

But these new cultivars would have been of little value without some means of replicating them and of getting them into field use. That is the task of extension.

---

[27] Or, in the case of Bangladesh, rice with immensely long stalks. These enable the plant to grow even in the very deep water which covers the paddy fields at flood time, and then fold down as the floods pass and the water evaporates. Agriculture is rarely straightforward.

The extensionists are, for my money, the heroes in the fight against world poverty. They are the guys who take on the seemingly impossible job of taking some promising new plant variety from research to field use. This involves empathy with the farmers, great management skills, immense persuasiveness and conviction, and abounding energy. Sometimes in the face of severe physical and psychological hazards, as we will see in South Kordofan in the Sudan.

Research often hits snags which, with hindsight, seem obvious. The KONGWA (Knocked Out No Good Wasted Agric) groundnuts scheme in Tanzania is perhaps the most famous. But I hit one in the Yemen, as mentioned in the introduction. UN FAO had spent several years in the harshest of environments, the immensely romantic Hadramaut in the middle of the Arabian Deserts (Lawrence of Arabia's stamping ground). The city is composed astonishingly of five- and six-storey blocks – this is not irrelevant – made of sun-dried mud blocks. They look incredibly precarious, with great widening cracks stretching down entire floors. This is an old poster given me by Kalifa, whom I trained as computer manager. Precarious five story buildings often splitting apart vertiginously down the middle.

FAO developed their new rice variety to widespread plaudits. Short stalks, high quality, and high yield. But it was adopted not at all. Social anthropologists came in to find out why. The problem was that Yemeni rice had two functions: to feed people, and for the stalks to be used as straw for the mud bricks. And without stringy robust stalks of rice, the buildings would fall down.

But even given well-researched appropriate cultivars (seeds), the gulf between good trial plots in say, IRRI, the International Rice Research Institute in the Philippines, and successful production and harvesting in some remote part of the Third World, was often impassable. The cultivars have to be replicated in vast quantities in the target areas, the farming population have to be enthused and trained, the infrastructure has to be developed, e.g. access roads, granaries, transport, credit. It's an absorbing process which we'll look at further in the context of RISDA with smallholder rubber in Malaysia. There, a rubber tree's productive life is about twenty-five years, after which it has to be replaced. To do so a careful sequence of fifty-four actions were needed to get replanting carried out.

*

We saw in Chapter 4 a typical extensionist's safari in Uganda, visiting as many farms as could be fitted into a long day – usually only six to eight, because the visits need to be thorough and to be seen to be thorough. But, bearing in mind that the ratio of extensionists to farmers is sometime eight or nine hundred to one, these visits have to be very selective, often centring on demonstration plots or other training. One technique to enthuse the take up of new cultivars was to fence the trial plot in and visibly monitor it in the daytime. The smallholders sometimes came at night to get plants for their holdings!

The extensionists task in Malaysia for the Rubber Industry Smallholders Development Authority was much more varied and much more structured. The rubber tree's output of latex declines after it reaches 25 years old. So RISDAs primary objective is to assist the smallholders in replanting new trees, at a stage when, after many years tapping and processing their latex, they have to become farmers again. They have to cut down the old rubber, dispose of it or burn it, dig holes for the new trees, apply fertiliser, plant the new trees and care for them. At this stage the farmers show with pride bare ground with rows of tiny seedlings. The extensionists needs to visit, point out the wasted area where rain and solar radiation might be exploited, and propose as we did in Malaysia, interplanting with appropriate crops. This interplanting can continue for at least four years as the seedlings grow, and can be immensely effective. In our trials in Johor we helped to introduce several crops, including yams. The extensionists uncovered a very fruitful market across the border in Singapore close by.

That covers the extensionists interface with individual farmers. They also have major tasks in organising the processing of the latex in GPCs, group processing centres, where the latex is coagulated and rolled, smoked, and stamped for sale. They also coordinate the provision of inputs like fertilisers and pesticides and fungicides, and advise on the elimination of serious weeds, using for example lalicides. They also attend the fortnightly sales of the smoked rubber sheets, monitoring the bids for fairness, and occasionally stepping in and bidding if the buyers' offers are unfair.

The RISDA deputy Chief Extension Office, Said Barkat worked with us to set up the RISDA Action list for replanting., and the ones for interplanting various crops within the new rubber, e.g.:

GETAH   PENUTUP ASLI

RUBBER WITH CASSAVA

These would be used in two years of trials with 100 farmers in the far north, Kedah, and 100 in the far south, Johor.

These interplanting lists were to prove immensely important.

I like the Bahasa Malaysia language. The T in GETAH is almost spat out at you, as in traditional English, and in contrast with Essex English, or German, where the T is just a slovenly glottal stop. A hesitation, or a click in the throat. On the other hand, as we saw earlier, the ends of words like "Pink Form" were swallowed to become "Ping Fo".

Bahasa has another pleasing construct. For the plural you just say the singular twice. Laki is woman. Laki-laki is women. Bahasa Indonesia is very similar though not identical, so it's a widely used language.

While the Action Lists were being discussed with Replanting and Planning Divisions at KL, the Field Officers collected Profile data for the 200 participating farmers (this took a fortnight, during which I visited Indonesia, the start of an ongoing relationship with various projects, especially sugar). They bundled the profiles together and bussed them to us, and we set them up in one of the RISDA mainframes. Very exciting to see these long programmed-about documents now pouring in for processing for real.

Then we generated the reports for the first month of operation and took them out to Kedah and Johor. We visited the target nucleuses and watched the debates and actions which ensued. Then the completed reports, one for each monitored plot, went back for processing.

In the RISDA Action Lists, the definitions of the actions needed are non-trivial, and even in such a brilliantly run Authority, a lot of things can go wrong. The actions in RISDA start with the formal paperwork for actions and credit (the smallholders' consent is essential), then "slaughter-tapping" the old rubber (rubber trees decline rapidly in latex output after year 25 or so) using a chemical called Ethrel. This squeezes the final output of latex before the tree is cut down. Then chainsawing the trees; uprooting the stumps with a tractor; clearing and burning the vegetation; preparing the ground for the new seedlings; including PPK fertiliser; planting an intercrop or a cover crop and so on, until rubber tapping can start at year 8, when the farmer reverts to his normal tapping and processing activities. This all involves seventy-four actions by the farmer and the agencies concerned. To give just one:

64 – APPLY CCM11 FERTLISER FOR RUBBER PLANTS AT 80KG   31/10/81

OR 2 BAGS PER HECTARE USING .25KG PER TREE

The key characteristic to convey here is that the Scapa approach forced the planners and extensionists to describe arrangements precisely. In many Third World situations this is alleged to be impossible. It has to be understood how dependent the smallholders are on good information from a host of sources. Unless they have such assurance they are crippled, particularly in taking on new crops. This is one of the reasons why RISDA was so successful. It controlled much of the supply and marketing chain, and wielded such clout that it could influence suppliers outside the chain to do what was needed. That was why, against all conventional wisdom, their smallholders were able to outperform big estates like Dunlop, and gain a quarter of the entire world market.

However, after any success stand by while fate intervenes to biff you. The vibrant and radical new PM of Malaysia, Dr Mahathir Mohammed, had got involved in a debate with the UK as to whether Malaysia was a "developing nation", hence deserving UK aid, or whether it was now so developed as to stand on its own feet (the view from DFID). This got tangled up at one stage with the Concorde supersonic passenger jet project, which relied on a flight path down the Straits of Malacca (between Java and Malaysia) for its routes to the Far East and Australia to be economic. This would face Malay fishermen with an unpleasant sonic boom once a day. Mahathir Mohammed refused, the Brits in return stuck out for their suspension of aid, and MM then ruled publicly, as a guideline for purchases by Malays: "Buy British last". Not just government purchases – all purchases. Happily the Malaysians are a healthily sceptic nation as regards politicians, or this would have meant a grinding halt for us. Nevertheless it was an immense setback.

Dr Mohammed Nor's growing power base in RISDA with the 300,000 rubber farmers, for whom he was a national hero, worried the politicians. What if this immensely successful and charismatic figure resigned from RISDA and stood for Parliament? Various moves took place to undermine him, to attack his strategy which stamped on the corns of rival agencies like palm oil and the Min of Ag, and to suggest corruption in his dealings for the farmers. In the end he resigned. It was a sad loss for his country, and a blow for our support inside RISDA. To simplify the events which followed, Dr Nor was replaced on strange grounds. The SCAPA pilot system went ahead successfully, but the Ministry ruled that a simpler management system run by FELDA (Federal Land

Development Agency) should be adopted as standard.

However, the experience and results, publicised in a book by the UN's ILO (International Development Association) had an immense impact for the generality of smallholder management systems, e.g. in Malawi and Sri Lanka, to be covered in Issue 2.

Chapter 11
National Finance and Exploitation

Finance is an eyeball-glazing and snore-inducing subject, but it is of vital importance because it reflects the allegedly foremost motivation for imperialism. Is all the anguish about the Empire and Commonwealth countries exploiting or being exploited well founded? At the one extreme we have an official history of Bunyoro, which just states dismissively that "the proceeds of the poll tax were sent to England". True or false? Or did Uganda in fact receive a substantial Grant in Aid from the UK as stated in the annual budget? At the other end there are very sophisticated claims about the exploitation of previous colonies like Malaysia, India, or Uganda.

The key to the first, finance, is, I think, to look at the taxation system which most of the colonies and protectorates implemented. The second is to look at manufacturing and agriculture and see where and if exploitation occurred. A simple approach is to compare the way a typical coffee estate is managed now, 30 years after independence, with the way a similar estate was managed under colonial rule.

National Finances

In most British colonies, government, the Legislative Council, usually adopted the approach to national finances that had been developed over three centuries in the United Kingdom. During the approach to independence the colonial rulers in Uganda were trying to persuade the Ugandans to adopt many of the United States systems. For example the American constitution with its Senate and House of Representatives, the American practice for urban management, of a supreme autocratic City manager, as opposed to the British hierarchical sets of elected councils. Invariably the Ugandans took this proposal as an insult, holding it to suggest that they should accept something rather inferior.

"We must have the Westminster model."

The appendices on this subject include the front cover of the Government Uganda Accounts for 1959-65. Then a broad overview delivered by the Honourable CGR Melmoth, Minister of Finance of the production prospects for the nation in the coming year, and the suggested disposition of the Revenue. It is important to establish that this was not a system that died with Independence, so the similar survey for 1969 – seven years after independence, follows Boring, but vital to sound governance. And you would think that the detail and the scope and the terminology might come from any Commonwealth country, including the UK. Then a section is given dealing with the misty gritty of expenditure and income. Then the results of a survey of farm income. This was always difficult, and is still difficult in the 21st century – and often in developed countries as well. The smallholders' recollections of purchases and sales are often unknown or concealed, and few keep notebooks or records – in the sixties, few were literate. Interestingly, when it comes to taxation the chief criticism comes from the expats Ugandans paid a level of poll tax – tax per head – which for any middle-class household was trivial, whereas expatriates had to pay a level of 30% of their salaries in income tax.

Finally, far from "sending the poll tax to England", the UK made a substantial Grant in Aid to boost Uganda's revenues.

In the BBC Reith Lectures in 2012 the distinguished Cambridge professor, Niall Ferguson, put forward dramatic views on the nature of governments and how the world might avoid the catastrophic future that the recent 100 Group of nations forecast to be likely. Ferguson identified a key problem area, the need for appropriate institutions. He dates the British success in developing these institutions from the glorious Revolution of 1688, when the Dutch King, William of Orange, and his English wife Mary started a process of institutional development which transformed the country. Democratic elections, the rule of law, cabinet government, the convention of cabinet responsibility (where the entire Cabinet is bound by any joint decision), independent commercial practice.

I disagree diffidently, in that I would date the key developments back earlier, to Tudor times, the 1530s. I well remember as a student in Cambridge, perched at the giddy top of an ancient steeply sloping lecture theatre, "Old Anatomy", looking down on the prematurely balding black-fringed head of the young Prof GR Elton as he explained the workings of the Tudor Treasury.[28] How did they record safely transactions between tax payer and Treasury so that there could be firm evidence if it came to a dispute? The answer is "tallies". The taxpayer came to the Treasury with the taxes available in gold and silver, and at handover a chunk of wood, a tally, was split in half, each party retaining a half which if needed could be compared with the other. The tally was often marked off in notches, sometimes in marks of five, each group with a line through it to ease computation. The procedures fascinated me, and led me later to pursue a career in systems analysis when I joined International Computers. This led to thirty fascinating years as a consultant and programmer in UN's FAO (Food and Agricultural Organisation), UK Department for International Development and the World Bank, and a view of

---

[28] Professor Sir Geoffrey R Elton, *The Tudor Revolution in Government*, Cambridge University Press, 1953. He saw the development of these key institutions as the autonomous actions of human agents, threading their way to viable procedures.

how these procedures, originated in Tudor England, dominated worldwide.

Exploitation

When I first arrived in Uganda I had the immense pleasure of buying my first car, and being a patriotic Brit, I went for a Standard Vanguard, a robust estate with high ground clearance and a Ferguson tractor engine specially designed for thumping Third World driving. I contracted to pay £800. I then toiled up the hill from Twentsche Motors, the Dutch importers, to the Treasury where a Mr Da Silva, lean and arrogant, refused to authorise the purchase. Down the hill again to see Twentsche and they dropped the price by £100. Up the hill again in the blazing tropical heat to which I was not yet acclimatised to see Mr Da Silva again. Dripping with sweat and hope! I sought his approval. No-go. Down the hill again, and Twentsche dropped another hundred pounds. Up again, and at last I got my car. But I felt continually in my five years with Uganda government that:

Why, when we are subsidising the Uganda Protectorate, do we Brits not get some preferential treatment? But it was a level playing field for all nations, and the French dominated the automobile field with their Peugeot 403, the Italians the fuel field with Agip.

As we will see later, the term "Imperial preference" meant preferential status, low import duties into the UK, to Empire and Commonwealth countries. Derided by Paxman but vital to the countries concerned. And for many, e.g. the Sudan and the West Indies, this Imperial preference was vital to their smallholders' economic success, against for example in the West Indies the massive, mechanised banana estates run by US firms like Dole and Chiquita on the South American mainland. In the UK schools you still find teachers who tell their pupils that the preference meant that Commonwealth countries were compelled to buy from the UK, and that their classes should feel guilt for their history. In fact the reverse was true.

Chapter 12

The Scrombles – Whatifs – The Previous Government Syndromes – The Devonshire Course

This chapter covers the myths and realities of the notorious scrambles, the "previous government" syndromes, and then the training course we were given. The course gives an idea of the objectives of the Empire and Commonwealth from the 1920s on. This was the period when the great transition to western civilisation took place.

*

The great British journalist James Cameron gives a pleasing description of the command which the Dutch use to order their troops to mount their horses:

"Scromble op die beesties."

It reminds me of the conventional view of the scrambles for Africa, India, and South East Asia and Oceania as an unprincipled onslaught and carve-up. Alluded to for example by Neil Oliver. It's only partly true. But in any case, in my view for what it's worth, no attempt of any significance has been made to suggest a better, quicker way of bringing civilisation to the African continent in particular. No attempt at a WhatIf? No simple spreadsheets. You need to read Colonel Thruston's account of his time with the Baganda in the 1890s to get a view of the savagely violent truth.

Buganda's wealth then was based on war, slavery, and ivory. East Africa of the 19th century has been described as a "maelstrom of warring tribes", and there is little reason to suppose that this maelstrom would have developed through the thousand years of civilising which separated it from 19th-century Europe except as a result of the allegedly infamous "Scramble".

Until 1881 the European powers were reluctant to develop any involvement in this formidably hostile continent. They were driven into it by commercial considerations and pressures from their nationals in the area concerned and from religious and liberal pressures, e.g. to abolish the slave trade, as we have seen developing in Uganda. But in the case of the British, much of the African Empire until then was "created in a fit of absent mindedness", under pressure from the likes of Cecil Rhodes, whose ideal of an Africa developed by the Brits from Cape to Cairo was immensely powerful, and by the Victorian missionaries, like David Livingstone, and notably the CMS – Church Missionary Society. It was strongly opposed by politicians like the Gladstonian Liberals.

But by 1880, Count Otto von Bismarck in the rising state of Germany dominated European policy. This dominance was born of the Prussian state's flowering under Frederick the Great and Wilhelm 1. And in 1881, for no clear reasons, Bismarck resolved to reverse his antipathy to empire – "I am no man for colonies." – and started instead a scramble for territory which other European powers rapidly followed. They would send missions or similar groups to establish a presence in an area, then extend outward to reach a boundary with another scrambling nation.

The scramble has generally being castigated as a ruthless exercise in drawing straight lines across the maps of the entire continent and this is in most cases true. But usually there were no established borders. In some cases the process has been disastrous. The best example I know of is the shape: on the map of the Sudan, which encompassed both the vast

Islamic desert empire based on Khartoum and also a massive part of sub-Saharan Africa inhabited by Nilotic tribes like the Nuer and Dinka. Tribes who looked different from the aquiline northerners, had nothing in common culturally with them, and were treated like slaves. The resulting country, the largest in Africa, has recently been split up after a thirty-year war, into Sudan and South Sudan. If readers would like an impression of the Nuer and Dinka tribes in the 1940s, a description by the anthropologist, Evans Prichard, is both true and immensely entertaining. But coupling these warring and completely undeveloped tribes onto the Sudanese state proved to be a disaster.

So how should the partitioning operation to create viable units and nations have been done? The finest example of British imperialism for me was the Molson Commission, which was described in Chapter 3. But that was in the last years of the Ugandan Protectorate, in 1963. It was a very expensive study carried out by three Lords of the Privy Council, with all the support which modern communications, air transport, settled administration, trained interpreters and so on, provided. A very costly method of resolving a dispute covering just eleven counties. And we are talking of the largest continent on earth, with countless such counties. And even then the British government kicked the ball into touch, leaving the issues raised by the Molson Commission to be decided on by the new independent Uganda Government. Anyone like Tony Benn who maintains that democracy should have been used to carve up Africa in the 1890s is clearly unaware of what was then feasible – to put it politely. And to carry out such an enterprise across all of Africa in the 1890s? Central Africa in the 1880s was a "shifting warring, slaving maelstrom of different tribes, cultures and languages". Bridging between this 10th-century environment[29] and the 20th

---

[29] If you compare the social organisation in Kigezi and other features like the land apportionment system to those in England in the tenth century the similarities are relevant.

century was never going to be easy, and boundaries and linkages, however straight and arbitrary, were perhaps the best route in. The indignation of historians like Simon Schama against the "scramble" provoke the Yorkshire school playground response:

"Well; and what would you have done then, clever clogs?"

Niall Ferguson, perhaps our finest historian, points out that the world economy grew faster between 1870 – the start of the scramble – and 1913 than in any previous period.[30]

The idea that the Empire was fundamentally brutally military also seems suspect. Professor A.L. Kennedy gives the sizes for the various European armies in 1840. That of the Brits is roughly the same as that of the Austrians. You don't rule a quarter of the planet with 240,000 troops unless you have the tacit consent, in the philosopher John Locke's terms, of those who are ruled.

In practical terms, there was no oppressive military activity in Uganda when I was there. We saw the Fourth KAR (Kings African Rifles) only on their annual recruiting safaris, when we were keenly and, tragically, unavailingly trying to persuade the southerners to join to keep a tribal balance.

There are examples which militate in the opposite direction, i.e. in favour of a rough partition, a rough "scramble" with loose, exploratory boundaries, as was actually imposed. The swiftest means perhaps of getting the benefits of civilisation to the regions concerned.

For me the most striking example of this is that of the tragic recent history of Rwanda. Rwanda's boundaries were decided early in the 20th century, and fairly accurately matched the boundaries of the two existing kingdoms of Rwanda and Burundi.[31] Did these boundaries wall their peoples in

---

[30] *The War of the World*, page 16, Niall Ferguson, Penguin Group, 2008.
[31] Insert a description of Purcell and the white fathers.

disastrously? I was fortunate to be ADC of the county immediately north of the Rwanda border in Uganda. The same tribal allegiances pertained as led in Rwanda to one million deaths. But in Bufumbira there was only an immense concern at the events across the border, and shelter was readily given to refugees.

A key reason for the Rwandan genocide is alleged to be that it resulted from the Belgians supporting the Tutsi rulers and propagating the idea that they were, like the pastoralist Abel in Genesis, racially superior and predestined to rule over the crop farming Hutu, the sons of Cain. But the differences went far deeper than could have been achieved in a short European domination.

What about basic tribal hostility as a reason for the genocide? There certainly was a propensity for the two tribes to show rivalries, as I found in Uganda. The Tutsi were invading cattle keepers from the North, and had imposed their rule over maybe six centuries on the arable farmers, the Hutu. However, in the Ugandan county of Bufumbira, with the same tribal mix, the government saw the growing pressure on land, which occurred on both sides of the border. Too much peace! But in Uganda we were able by voluntary and happy resettlement of people in the game plains to find empty land for the youngsters. (I pointed out this key socio-economic dimension to some journalists from the Sunday Broadsheets. Only Andrew Marr had the commitment to reply, broadly agreeing.)

I remember one of the barazas held by Gus Ferguson, the resettlement officer, and the Mutwale, the County Chief. Seen here with Walter Baumgartel below Muhavura volcano.

POST-COLONIAL HOKUM

Graphic from "Konig in Gorillaland", Walter Baumgartel, W Keller and Co, Stuttgart 1960.

The barazas were a great occasion for amusement, stories about the elephants and lions in the resettlement area chasing the old warrior. The Mutwale, Paulo Rukeribuga, sported medals from the Germans, when he fought an epic war in WW1 under the great General Von Lettow Vorbeck, and medals from the Brits in WW2. He dominated his people, keeping a wife in each significant area of the county – no doubt they had their ears to the ground and briefed him as he toured. He married a young lady from Rwanda, a dynastic match as in 16th-century Europe, and then contracted prostate cancer. He wouldn't accept operation, and died as he had lived, widely mourned. Better dead than impotent. My interpreter in Hoima, a very genial guy, explained how he ran his marriage, also to four wives. "I stay each night with a different wife so as to prevent jealousy. And they always eat before me from the pot in case the food is poisoned."

The Bufumbira settlers were moved 80 miles to the game plains to see the area and plots, which were being marked out 10 acres each. Water was laid on, a school was being built, and agricultural extension and health services were well advanced. It was a strikingly happy development, and much of the resettlement I saw elsewhere was very popular.

So why did the tragedy of Rwanda not repeat itself in this part of Uganda which had the same mix of tribes? The answer I suggest is that the penning into the maps of the boundaries of Rwanda, however successful and accurate they were at the time, constrained any response to the swiftly growing population's need for free land. So drawing lines on a map could sometimes be disastrous, and the carve-up of the 1880s, the infamous "scramble" may have been simple and often effective response. No maps were possible of most of Africa then, but the example of contemporary India is relevant. The map from DK Fieldhouse's *The Colonial Empires* shows India in the time of the princely states, a muddled, numerous, and complicated mixture.[32] Left alone, it seems unlikely that the great nation of India would have evolved.

---

[32] Fieldhouse, DK. *The colonial empires*, MacMillan 1986, p194.

How would the much-loved national railway system for example, have been developed? What about land titles for farmers without the Indian Survey? The list would be long and exhausting. The same sort of muddle which caused the French Revolution in 1789.

The lessons are important. Some countries like Zambia have vast areas of cultivable land – only 10% in use. To resettle people across from Rwanda into these open farmlands might be a key solution. This I found with a friend, Jean-Marie Mukandilla, when touring the farms in Zambia, is actually happening on an individual basis despite governmental obstacles firmer even than those we impose on immigration into the UK.

Chapter 13
Agricultural Management

On a Tuesday in April, 1978 I walked down the street from London's Victoria tube station towards the Overseas Development Administration (now DFID) in Eland Place. A blustery wind, sky studded with white clouds on the blue, daffodils already a-flower in Grosvenor Gardens. With a lifting heart I recalled a serendipitous concert yesterday evening, when I wandered to Westminster embankment and then chanced on the final, celebratory concert of this year's graduands from the Royal College of Music in the Queen Elizabeth Hall across the river.

The Thames' flood tide flowing past the South Bank terraces, rippling into wavelets against a vigorous northwester. Into the hall, to hear Prokofiev's Classical Symphony, a splendidly light, exuberant vehicle for youth and for the feelings of the occasion. Admiring and loving audience of parents and friends. Themes thrown with a passing smile from flute to bassoon to clarinet, classmates in three years' musical journeyings, celebrating with joy their friendship and intense application. A snatch of civilisation unsurpassed.

Meanwhile, as I walked, I ran over in my mind the key points in the coming meeting. How far could the project (SCAPA, System for Computer-aided Agricultural Planning and Action) be held to fit the ministry's guidelines? The splendidly altruistic approach of Judith Hart's White paper *More Aid for the Poorest* had survived largely unscathed through the years. But how far would it really be followed under the free-enterprise ethos of Thatcherism? Would its leading-edge aspects be an attraction? To the politicians perhaps, yes. But to the bureaucrats who made the decisions, who can tell?

I passed the entrance to Force Four Chandlers and into Eland Place, and my mind trundled off down a siding familiar to boat owners in the springtime – more varnish and antifouling needed? What about the echo sounder and those funny random numbers which suddenly appeared and suggested alarming shallows in the middle of the Irish Sea? No, no time to go in to the shop now.

I pushed through the glass doors into Eland House and declared my business.

"I'm with Professor Black and Dr Leakey. I'll wait here if you don't mind until they come."

"All right, dear. But don't lose the pass, mind, or we won't be able to let you out."

Leakey arrived after 15 worrying minutes. As usual before key meetings he was sharp and alert; a restless and demanding companion.

No sign of Black. Leakey was uneasy:

"Hope Gordon's not up to one of his devices. If I doesn't show up, perhaps you'd like me to introduce the project?"

I felt robust. It was going to be a good day. My project after all, wasn't it? These two had contributed a lot, but ICL's (International Computers) stamp on the whole thing had to be maintained.

"No, that's OK," I said confidently. "You can come in when we get to questions."

"Well, if you're sure." Leakey sounded doubtful.

We talked over the White paper issues until interrupted.

"Mr Stutley will see you now."

We reached room H54. P. Stutley, Chief Natural Resources Advisor.

*

Stutley greeted us and introduced two colleagues whose names I missed. One, the dark-haired one, looked smooth and urbane, the administrator perhaps. The other, blond, had a broad, flat brow wrinkled with concern and the physique of a rugger player. Wing forward perhaps in my time. Disarming, honest face. Kept in the background. All had the courteous, slightly withdrawn watchfulness of senior civil servants when in contact with industry. Stutley kicked off:

"My role is that of so-called expert." He glanced at them quizzically. Both Leakey and I knew the 'so-called' to be uncalled-for. In our background research Stutley's name had several times cropped up as the incisive author of monographs or whatever on this or that aspect of rural development. No doubt Stutley knew that we knew that, but nevertheless he took evident pleasure in enlarging on his role, his deep concern to verify the theoretical content and quality of the project, and his total inability, as one who was strictly an advisor, to do anything or decide anything whatsoever. He would place his views on record for those who decide in these matters to take a decision at the stage at which it was appropriate for a decision to be taken.

I felt anchored to my seat as if by a puddle of brown sticky porridge. The contrast with the sharp action-focused development review meetings in ICL was total. Thirty or so key managers at the weekly review, each with a few short seconds to defend his people and patch.

"You committed to deliver issue 3.1.5 of the microcode for the SCU at the start of week 17. Is it delivered?"

"No, because..."

"I'm not interested in excuses. That project's a can of worms. Did you raise an Orange Alert? What recovery action have you taken?"

Here in the ministry I was out of my depth, feeling I was among people who were stringing together familiar words, but producing language whose real meaning was elusive and yet immensely important. And well-understood, moreover, by everyone else present.

I embarked on a description of the SCAPA system, concentrating on its value in supporting small farmers and extensionists in introducing new varieties of major cash crops. I quoted one source, Coleman, on whose ideas we had particularly leant.

"Coleman," said the dark one suspiciously. "Isn't he an American? Harvard, I think I remember."

I continued nervously, quoting another source.

"Giddings. Another American. Also from Harvard, I think," interrupted the dark guy severely.

"Yes," said Stutley uneasily, "I think you're right. Not that..."

"No, of course. But you know **ESCOR**, Peter. What would ESCOR say for God's sake? Still," he said kindly, "do carry on, Mr er... Total."

I felt my audience slipping, their eyes glazing, their watch arms twitching. I went on to describe the project briefly; why ICL had taken it up; how the university came into it; why, despite the fact that the proposals were high-tech and did not come from typical sources for new DAA proposals for overseas development – e.g. Oxford, Reading, Norwich, Sussex – they merited funding.

"Yes," said the second guy, the black-haired fellow, "we've read the papers carefully, haven't we, Peter. But our feeling really, given the absence, and this is crucial of course, of a request from a Third World country, and bearing in mind the weight of deserving and immediately appropriate..."

Leakey chipped in quickly: "If I may just interject. I think it might be helpful to you, gentlemen, since Mr Tottle comes from a discipline with which you and I are unfamiliar, if I amplify a little on how these suggestions strike me as a simple, practical man. Like me you are perhaps strangers to the particularities of these arcane avenues of recent computing research."

He smiled warmly, persuasively at each. Stutley glanced with raised eyebrows at the dark-haired guy. He nodded.

Leakey then entered a light-hearted but exciting justification for the proposal. Like many whose brains work very fast, he had the unconscious habit of repeating phrases with swift paraphrases in a tumbling rhythm which was elusive and invigorating. People had to listen hard just to keep up. Leave alone interrupt.

The university/ICL research, he outlined, had revealed this possible fresh route to development.

The funding aspect was not vital – ICL could trivially fund the task from its own budgets, but the external imprimatur of the ministry, its seal of approval, was vital if the normal accusations from the media and elsewhere were not to stick –

allegations of commercial motivation and exploitation for example – and if the necessary extent of cross-disciplinary collaboration inside universities and industry and between institutions was to be achieved.

"Those among us," Leakey continued, "whose arteries are not yet hardened," a beaming, re-assuring smile made it clear that the present company were numbered among those whose arteries were indubitably youthful, "see the vitally important and constructive role this sort of initiative can play at the leading edge of technology."

The civil servants relaxed. Stutley began to probe with a few questions.

At this stage there was an urgent knock at the door.

"Professor Black, Mr Stutley." Stutley's PA appeared, but was suddenly and startlingly replaced by the tall burly figure of Professor Black.

"Mu-my dear chuch-chap,"

Black came in, his right hand eagerly and warmly out-thrust at Stutley, his coat, hat, and briefcase hugged precariously under his left arm.

"Su-ho nice to meet you at last. I'm mu-most awfully su-su-su-su-horry. Those Manchester tut-trains. The 7.53 as usual you know." Black stammered out some apologies.

"No, no, Professor, delighted…"

The civil servants seemed bemused, sympathetic and immensely deferential.

"H engine bub-bub."

"We're delighted to have you here."

They mustered to help the professor sort himself and his coat and his hat and his papers out. They sat anxiously alert while he painfully expressed his views. A most praiseworthy Bub-Bub-Bu-British initiative. The stammering was sometimes quite harrowing. Black's tongue would twist and lollop distressingly in and out of his mouth like a purple epileptic serpent.

Outside distant drums and fifes approached, increasingly loud.

"We cuc-cuc-cu-han't be left behind."

"The Scots Guards," explained Stutley quietly; the civil servants were clearly accustomed to the din. The band came closer. The guards' boots crunched and echoed dramatically below, the insistent rattle of the kettle drums drawing Leakey's pencil to tap in time. Black entered into a long description of how he had as a budding researcher in the late 50s, publicly declared his own field, computing, to be a specialists' backwater. Massive number crunching, weather forecasting, nuclear physics, artillery range tables. Not much else. World demand for computers by 2000 in the region of seventeen machines.

"How wrong cu-cu-cu-han you be?" he concluded with rueful humility. "How r-r-r-hong can you be?"

The civil servants looked warmly respectful. Takes a big man to recount his blunders.

Might it not be so, suggested Black, with this current proposal? So easy to reject the far-sighted in favour of the conventional. To select with tunnel vision the meticulously presented Price-Gittinger[33] conformant pap, and let the seeds of the future float by. Stutley smiled sympathetically. The Scots Guards gradually receded towards the memorial. The fresh leaves on the plane trees shone green and translucent in the sunshine. I relaxed, delight suffusing my veins.

We've done it, I thought. *We've done it. We're going to win after all.*

---

[33] Price Gittinger's work was then the template for development project proposals.

Stutley stressed again the informative and advisory nature of his role. He should not initiate. But sometimes, for Third World countries, there was a need for pump-priming. He might prime the pump.

They discussed the plan, who might go to Winban when, when they might come back, budget, allowances, insurance. Stutley emphasised the importance of having a social anthropologist in the team to get at the real motivation of the smallholders, as against that which they said they espoused.

They talked further over the ministry's protocols and procedures.

"But what about ESCOR?" asked Leakey, troubled about the attitude of this mysterious committee.

"Oh, Humphrey will take care of ESCOR," said Stutley. His dark-haired colleague smiled with easy, lofty, enigmatic confidence. These two were pulling the strings in the best of ways. But they weren't the **well-meaning men in dark suits and black felt hats, with neatly rolled umbrellas crooked over the left forearm, who were imposing their constipated view of life** as alleged by Orwell and Paxman.

The Manchester three later surrendered their passes and came out of the ministry doors.

"Dr-hink and a bu-bite?" suggested Black.

"Good idea."

Leakey looked carefully around and behind them as we strode fast and cheerfully to the pub.

"Gordon," he said to Black, "that was magnificent. Confess now, the Mu-Mu-Mu-Mu-Hanchester train was actually spot on-time, wasn't it now?"

Black's face reddened and swelled up into a massive schoolboy grin, uncontainably pleased with himself, unable to squeeze his pleasure into the habitual sober cast of academic propriety. We all hugged ourselves with delight.

People may question my description of Gordon Black. But for me he typifies the capacity of humans not only to surmount their severest impediments, but to use them. Many of his admirers used to think that Gordon's stammer was sometimes exaggerated deliberately. I doubt it. But it proved immensely effective, notably in meetings. Everyone would hang on desperately while the words eventually came out, and this tortuousness interrupted the normal flow of discourse very tellingly and persuasively. He once had me to lunch at Manchester University, and described how tough it had been for him, on his own, on a recent government-contrived month's tour of China. You can imagine his difficulty stammering out his ideas in a totally different culture. Particularly the Chinese. As we were to find in the eighties, they surround you from dawn to beyond dusk with immensely intelligent hosts, who suck every last ounce of thought from you until at the end of a day you are bemused and exhausted. And all in the most courteous and persuasive manner possible.

I asked Colin Leakey recently, from his time at Makerere University (then the University for East Africa) about research allegedly being confined to the cash crops – supposedly showing the Brits' obsession with colonial exploitation.

He responded: "Graham, remember that 'Protectorate' times were before Makerere became independent of London University. 'Agriculture' at that time at Makerere did absolutely no research whatever. After independence and a few years later when freeing itself from London University, there was then a start to agricultural research at the University Farm. So far as I know, until 1973 anyway, there was no research there on cotton, and sugar. Almost all was on food crops including sweet potatoes (Andrew Macdonald) and on legume pulses and oil seeds (my group and with support from soils science and folk working nearby at Namulonge. l had published on coffee and on cotton from work done before I left Government to join Makerere. At Makerere we published indeed on vanilla (a 'food' crop? and on cocoa diseases). So the account of which you write is substantially bunk! Colin." For the present, suffice it to say that the SCAPA project continued from the above beginnings to be discussed widely and established in several countries in the Commonwealth as we will see later.

Chapter 14
Environment and Wildlife

After my second safari in Bufumbira, I resolved to climb mount Muhavura, the 13,500ft. volcano sometimes known to the Bakiga as the Rainmaker, sometimes as The Guide, because on nearly every hill top, up to fifty miles away, you could see the triangular summit and steer by it. This was at the first Rwanda crisis in 1960, when we anticipated a breakdown of law and order in the Congo or Rwanda and we prepared to repel invasion and accommodate refugees. We feared that the Rwandans would swing their armies north round the seven great volcanoes and through Uganda for an easy surprise attack on the towns Goma and Rutshuru in the Congo. I represented the civil authority, and was with a platoon of the 4th KAR, Kings African Rifles, encamped outside the Kisoro township and in trenches looking down on the border post. They were led by a British National service subaltern, and included a certain Sgt. Idi Amin, Uganda's heavyweight boxing champion and future president.

I had a dodgy special radio link over the mountains to Kabale, radio unheard of in those parts, and I delighted in exercising the procedures familiar from my service in the Royal Signals. Changing frequency at dusk for example, to accommodate the changing skip distance to Kabale as the heavyside layer moved away from the earth and our signals bounced back from it but farther off. The guy at Kabale didn't even appreciate the need to terminate each phrase with 'over', so we had long pauses! V bombers were said to be on standby in Cyprus or Kenya.

Idi Amin and his platoon being led by Graham up Mt Muhavura, 13500 ft.

We were led off up the mountain at 0400, and made good time to the Saddle camp at 10,000 ft., still in the bamboo. This fascinated me, and I'd heard of the rare mountain gorilla. I looked at Reuben and he grinned.

"Maybe we come back here Bwana?"

"Ndio." Yes, I replied – one of the few words in Swahili I knew. We toiled on up the great slag heap. Eventually the soldiers tired, unused and sickened at the altitude, and Reuben and I climbed on alone to the summit. A small volcano top pool surrounded by the rim. You could have looked down on Tanzania, Uganda, Congo, Rwanda, and Burundi. And the Speke peak of the Mountains of the Moon 200 miles away, but for the mist. But I resolved to climb all three volcanoes if Reuben would take me – he was, as the Game guard, Bufumbira, opening up a track through the realms of the gorilla. They at that time were still regarded as fearsomely savage, capable of tearing humans apart – and of course quite strong enough to do just that.

The gorillas' bad press was not improved a year later when a Japanese research group followed them with Reuben's guidance. They heard the famous drumming noise, and the lead male gorilla thumped his chest violently and charged at them, teeth bared, downhill.

They dived sideways as he came at them, but one was slashed nastily across the chest and had to be carried down 4,000 feet. Not an Attenborough moment!

I was fortunate to climb the other two volcanoes, Mgahinga and Sabinio with Reuben. Over many years he opened up a few tracks through the virgin jungle, and guided future research teams, especially George Schaller. His activities also held back the farmers who were encroaching higher and higher on the steep flanks of the mountains, clearing the bamboo to get at the fertile black soil which had been deposited over millennia. Soil which had been held together by the root systems, and would now, as the root structures decayed, slide away thousands of feet in the torrential rains.

Hugh Fraser, the DC, felt the guy had made an "incredible contribution to civilisation", and undeniably had helped preserve the few remaining mountain gorilla as a species. His life had been at risk from the poachers, and the fearsome wildlife, particularly buffalo – no lions at that altitude. Working alone high in those vast mountains – no one would have missed him or could have found him if he had been injured. Hugh resolved to get him the OBE (Order of the British Empire). Rarely has it been more merited.

Graphic from "Konig in Gorillaland".

POST-COLONIAL HOKUM

Reuben Rwanzagire, Game Guard
OBE

Graphic from "Konig in Gorillaland". This is what the Commonwealth was all about.

Chapter 15

Culture, Language, and Sport

This is a topic which I approach with great diffidence because it is so sprawling and so stunning.

However, in sport I did as a result of training in the Royal Signals, with great distance runners of the early 50s, Ken Norris and Fred Ranger – 40 miles a week on the North Yorkshire Moors – gain great pleasure in athletics. We won the British army cross-country championships. So after arrival in Kabale, I agreed to chair the Kigezi Athletics Association. I soon found the Bakigas' track and cross-country capability daunting. Every year, in the years I was involved, the Kigezi District Championships produced yet another brilliant long-distance runner, at times easily bettering those achieved at Oxford and Cambridge in my time. And that was just after Chataway and Brasher had taken Bannister to his great mile record at Iffley Road, Oxford, when he broke the four-minute barrier. So chairing the district Athletic Association for a couple of years and helping with administration was for me an immense pleasure. The great Ugandan athlete Stephen Kipritich has just won the 2012 Olympic marathon, but he was from the east. We have yet to see the Bakiga triumph – perhaps in the Commonwealth marathon in 2014.

Sailing Olympics 2012 – Weymouth immensely friendly sunny but windless. Crowds draped happily round the great headland of the Note.

As regards languages, we had a great privilege on the Devonshire Course of being taught by Snoxall, who collaborated in writing then the definitive Luganda dictionary. And when I went to Kigezi I found Brian Kirwan had written the Runyankore/Rukiga grammar, including a splendid variety of the great chiga proverbs, for example:

"*Mpora mpora ekahitsya ekinyangondokyera aha iziba.*"

Illustrating the causative. *Ekahitsya*, to cause something to arrive somewhere. *Hika* reach. *Okuhika*, the infinitive, to reach. *Okuhitsya*, to cause something to reach somewhere. *Ekyokuhitsya*, the thing which causes something to reach somewhere.

In English, "Slowly slowly gets the earthworm to the well." The tortoise beats the hare. More haste, less speed.

A grammar as complex as Latin, with up to 14 noun

classes, and all somehow evolved throughout the hundreds of Bantu languages of sub-Saharan Africa without benefit of any conscious discussion or written script, orthography. Gradually mapped, according to Noam Chomsky, onto the universal Transformational Grammar, a structure which is in a child's brain from birth or even earlier.

Astonishing. Mind bending. Indicative, subjunctive, imperative, reflexive, passive, active, far future, future, present continuous, present, imperfect, perfect, pluperfect. And that's just the verbs. Most Brits nowadays would be at a loss to understand all this as their language and grammar crumbles away rather like Chinese. No prepositions, no subjunctives. And historians have to use only one tense, the present. I teach visiting Germans occasionally, and they quiz me about English grammar rules and constructs as they've been taught them. Rules which I can't understand – we've lost them.

Many years later I was trained in linguistics as part of a TEFL qualification – teaching English as a foreign language. The linguistics prompted me to go further into the amazing range of grammars which we encountered in Uganda and in nearly all of sub Saharan Africa.

A conclusion from all this: Critics of the Empire and Commonwealth lack the imagination to see how vital the cultural aspects were to civilising the communities concerned. The interest in all this, i.e. linguistics, is said to have originated in one of the great clubs in Calcutta in the 1820s. Then some members, fascinated by Indian culture, noticed the similarities between Hindi and English, and started tracking them back via Latin and Greek to what proved to be a common stem, Sanskrit, emerging in 1600 BC.

Chapter 16

Law and the Commonwealth

As a general view of the Commonwealth and its fifty-four countries readers may like to visit its website:

www.thecommonwealth.org

To quote the fundamentals:

History:

The association has roots as far back as the 1870s. It was reconstituted in 1949 when Commonwealth Prime Ministers met and adopted the 'London Declaration' where it was agreed all member countries would be "freely and equally associated."

Beliefs and Values:

The Commonwealth believes the best democracies are achieved through partnerships – of governments, business, and civil society.

Beyond the ties of history, language and institutions, members are united through the association's values of: democracy, freedom, peace, the rule of law and opportunity for all.

These values were agreed and set down by all Commonwealth Heads of Government at two of their biennial meetings (known as CHOGMs) in Singapore in 1971 and reaffirmed in Harare in 1991.

The values are protected at government level by the Commonwealth Ministerial Action Group (CMAG), a rotating group of nine Foreign

Ministers, which assesses the nature of any infringement and recommends measures for collective action from member countries. It can suspend or recommend to Heads of Government that a member country be expelled. When countries are suspended, the Commonwealth makes every effort to bring them back into the fold.

As students, after three years of study, we were taught that, there were just two **vital** principles of good government and a good life:

Democracy and the Rule of Law

The rule of law has often been a major reason for the Empire and Commonwealth's appeal to its member peoples, and for obvious reasons, some of which I have touched on, such as security of title for smallholder farmers, security of contract for industrial and commercial organisations. The list would be long and perhaps tedious.

I give one example below, quoting their website, about the lawyers. With reservations – there is a current quip in the UK:

"The rule of law is being replaced by the Rule of Lawyers, so beware!"

"The Commonwealth Lawyers' Association (CLA) is an international organisation which exists to promote and maintain the rule of law throughout the Commonwealth by ensuring that an independent and efficient legal profession, with the highest standards of ethics and integrity, serves the people of the Commonwealth. Lawyers have much to learn from the comparative experience of other Commonwealth countries and share substantial common ground in their legal systems, education and practice. In the pursuit of these objectives, the CLA participates in a wide range of activities including advocacy, undertaking research projects, organising the biannual Commonwealth Law Conference and providing

services to our members."

As nations voyage into the future, a future abounding with promise and abounding with peril, the capacity to interact at immensely detailed levels can be greatly valuable.

Chapter 17

Commonwealth Failures:

Iraq and Sudan

I worked in Iraq in 1990 as a UN specialist on agricultural databases, advising in Saddam's Planning Ministry, equivalent to the UK Treasury, the driving force of the country. We were in the massively fortified skyscraper, now rubble, which served as the heart of the Iraqi government. We worked high above the river three floors below Saddam's HQ suite, in the Dictator's Agricultural Planning Division. The fortifications were vastly more formidable than those of any US embassy – outside were extraordinary grey shutters, four inches thick, of hardened Posnan steel, 3 massive angled slabs of it for every office, wedges 30ft. by 5. They hung waiting the command, like crocodiles' eyelids, to blink away prowling missiles or tyrannicidal shells. An exciting and intimidating assignment.

Iraq's recent history included brief years as a member of the Empire, years which for my Iraqi friends were intense and familiar; but years of which, until my arrival, I had been hardly aware. Open discussion with them of issues like freedom, democracy and the rule of law – fundamentals of the Commonwealth – was very hesitant and oblique for obvious reasons, but they often referred back to the period of British rule and its procedures with affection.

Of the handful of foreigners allowed in to the ministry, I was the only westerner, admitted (reluctantly) as a United Nations Food and Agriculture Organisation (FAO) consultant to the Director of Agricultural Planning, Dr Dujaily, to help develop their sectoral database. It was a six-month assignment; three to analyse the requirements and develop the design, then a spell in Rome and the UK while the hard- and software were justified and procured, then three months implementation and training. It seemed a challenging project politically, culturally, and technically. I knew Iraq was vastly more advanced than the rest of Arabia, and remembered vaguely a horrific war with Iran and the recent execution of the *Observer*'s correspondent, Farzad Bazoft for photographing an airfield.

In Baghdad in June at noon it is hot. Fiercely hot. 47 degrees. And dry. Fiercely dry. Breathe in through your mouth quickly and you blister your gullet.

From the Dictator's office suite high up you can see most of the city. Two police Mercedes, a fading sun-battered green to the gunwales, topsides cream, dawdle truculently along Tigris Drive. The ancient river is low, a dirty, muddy, motionless brown. Even the water looks dry. Nothing else moves anywhere; everything crouches in dark corners, barely breathing, waiting for the sun to go away.

Three floors below, in the Dictator's Agricultural Planning Division, just alongside the lift shaft which the cruise missiles may home in on, I sat chatting with my Iraqi counterpart, Dr Hammadi. "Perhaps you would care to break your fast with me on Wednesday?" I suggested – it was Ramadan, and this flowery formula had been suggested to me as the done thing by the local FAO Projects officer. He had been right; the counterpart smiled with pleasure and said yes in an off-handed way – Iraqis are sparing about showing gratitude even though they feel it.

We were talking over the seminar on their new system which we would jointly give. The consultant planned to put up the age-old computing dictum GIGO – "Garbage in = Garbage out" – to pick out the vital importance of accuracy in the input data to the system. Get, say, the irrigation parameters wrong and you'll bring disaster on the farmers. Well, not disaster, they're not short on nous. But slightly wrong, and they might miss the error and suffer loss. I thought I would check that the Iraqis would understand "Garbage." Perhaps I should say "Rubbish." Put it to his colleague.

"No problyem," said the counterpart – a big, combative, courageous man, he was a mite touchy about his countrymen's grasp of English. "For sure they will understand either. Rubbish is small red root, white inside. Garbage is a round green vegetable size of a basket." My eyes gleamed with pleasure, but wisely I let it ride, resolving to look the two words up in my Arabic dictionary back at the flat. Or drop the analogy completely. On the hard disc of my PC spun the 1990 crop production data that were a key to the Gulf war – could Iraq stand out against sanctions, and for how long?

We concluded our discussion.

"See you later then."

"Right."

"Hello hello."

"Hello hello."

This was then their equivalent of a cheery goodbye.

Saddam's invasion of Kuwait took place on August 2nd 1990. I spent an uneasy night. What do you say to your friends and hosts the next morning when their country has suddenly gone berserk? I resolved to see Dujaily and to tell him the Iraqis were marching over a precipice. To make the point graphically I'd walk my fingers across his desk and over the edge.

I went in.

"Hallo Graham, take a pew." I sat opposite him. Next to Ahmed, a humorous young statistician who was discussing a spreadsheet on egg production with him. My back was to an open archway into the smaller adjoining office.

I launched agitatedly into my prepared spiel, saying I feared the Iraqis faced military disaster from the West. Then doing my finger-walking bit, to the edge of the desk and over.

Dujaily's face froze, then he behaved quite extraordinarily. He rolled his eyes violently and continuously from side to side. As he did so he ran into a long, heated tirade about Iraq's soldiery and rocketry, air force, secret weapons and so on – they were without question and for sure invincible. Ahmed looked sideways at me, crinkling his eyes, giving a very faint, quizzical, smile. I twigged and hastily backed off. I hadn't realised, I said, their technology was so advanced, and there were of course questions of Iraq's title to Kuwait and so on.

The tension eased; we chatted carefully and I left. As I did so, I glanced through the archway.

There I saw one of the sleekly dressed mystery men, but now in the military uniform of a full colonel. Dujaily's minder.

The United Nations debated the invasion and swiftly declared it illegal.

At this point things became serious. Saddam rounded up his 3,000 foreign "guests" shunting them around various hotels where they were held "for their safety".

A colleague, Nino Nicotra, Head of peach research at the Italian Research Institute near Rome, joined me in the city from the northern mountains. This made the whole operation more exciting and less alarming, particularly for an ex-historian like me. How would the world react to this unprecedented assault, exploiting 3,000 hostages, on International Law? (I guess now that if Saddam had not later released us hostages he would now still be Dictator of Greater Iraq-Kuwait.) We used to crouch on the rooftop below the parapet at night with our short-wave radios, listening intently to Margaret Thatcher "vomiting poison like a spotted serpent", as Saddam Hussein put it. We spent our days training local UN staff in Word and Lotus spreadsheets, designing a peach database which may still be in use in Rome, and practising take-offs from Saddam International airport using Microsoft Flight Simulator 4.

Graphic cartoon from Computer Weekly.

As things worsened, the UN decided to get us out.

We got clearance to cross the desert to Jordan in one of their Land Rovers, leaving Baghdad at 9am on 6th August. However, the driver protracted our departure (had to go home to see his wife, forty miles away for lunch) for 10 hours, so we arrived at the frontier post deep into the desert at 2am. I was mentally rehearsing my interview for the BBC at the border (they had a team there avid for news) when our driver came up with a broad smile. "We go back Baghdad," he said. The border had been closed at midnight. We slept on the rocky sand. A full moon, and I woke and considered setting off by foot for the 30-mile trek to the Jordan border. Not a good idea, though some had been reported to have succeeded, but others had been shot.

My escape plans foiled, I continued working in the ministry. The database I was working on looked very relevant to the UN sanctions and my thoughts turned to espionage.

I described the agricultural production database and a missile, which we had seen hidden under a motorway bridge on the way to Jordan, to the intelligence guy at the British Embassy. He was excited about the missile and took me to a splendid courtyard room, where we went through pictures to identify it. It was an "Al Abbas", and this provided the first concrete evidence that Iraq was moving armaments westwards to cover and later bombard Tel Aviv in Israel. Tel Aviv was later hit by several of these missiles. But he just thought the database "might be interesting". Actually it could have helped provide an answer to what became the key strategic issue of the war, how well Saddam could survive economic sanctions, what his food reserves were, and hence whether the 1991 war was necessary and could succeed. Though my opinion for what it's worth, is that sanctions were a no-go option. The Iraqis could easily double food production, and acquiring food from friendly countries would be no problem.

That night I thought about the lukewarm-ness of the intelligence guy towards the database, the dangers that spying posed to me and the team, and about abusing their friendship. Skulking around the corridors slipping spreadsheets of egg production and so on onto diskettes would undoubtedly be a beheading offence even for a Brit. As I have found on subsequent remote assignments, you get deeply involved with your colleagues, and take a highly partisan view of the world in their favour. I decided to do no more about the database.

Only gradually over the years have I come to realise quite how vicious was the blood-drenched regime – "below the ground mass graves, above the ground mass torture chambers" – and the risks Dujaily took, affecting not only him but his wife and family (for example, a night with one of Saddam's henchmen was often required of the wives of senior officials). Dujaily helped my two attempts to escape. Later Nino and I had a miserable evening at an Iraqi's house discussing a new proposal by our friends, to shunt us off for our safety to a special dry-lands rehabilitation project in the Western Desert as "essential specialists". Neither of us had any knowledge of hydro and that field. The temperature there, as in Baghdad in mid-summer is 47 degrees. Breathe in fast through your mouth and you blister your gullet.

The pressure intensified when UN Resolutions 661 to 664 instructed us hostages to withhold further work for the regime. These resolutions were debated at one of the regular meetings of the British community, about 200 present, held by Harold Walker, the British ambassador. Walker read out the UN's resolution instructing UN staff to withhold their labour, but was immensely cautious about giving it effect. When a clearly determined member of the audience asked, "Isn't this a matter of principle?" Walker affected a sort of surprise, and said, "Well... I suppose it might be regarded from that angle if one saw it that way." He was clearly worried by his recent experience attempting to prevent the beheading of the *Observer* reporter Farzad Bazoft.

I thought it over, and at the next meeting I said I'd withhold my labour. He said, "Oh I wouldn't do that. I wouldn't do that. I'll only have to come and try to dig you out of jail as I did Jennifer." (Bazoft's girlfriend.) He came over to me later, worried. "What did you say your name was?" I told him and he repeated his advice. "I'll only have to come and try to winkle you out of one of their jails, just like I did for Farzad Bazoft."

However, I did feel it was a matter of principle, and, at work the next day, when the Iraqi Minister refused permission to leave as and when I wished, I asked my Iraqi counterpart, Dr Hammadi, to come with me after work to FAO. There I asked for a meeting with the FAO Director and Nino also in attendance. I said that since my freedom had been denied I would work no more. Hammadi was deeply troubled. He assured me that I was perfectly safe. I could stay safely with him and his family as an honoured guest, they would love to have me. The big aggressive man almost grovelled to us. But I refused.

That night, at 2am, the police raided our apartments. Lights flashed, people screamed. I hid in an empty apartment across the landing. Had they come for me? When at last the screams died and the vehicles left, I moved back, but for a restless night. The next morning Nino and I resolved to get out somehow. We went and talked it over at FAO, and they offered us sanctuary in their building. By day we stayed in the two-storey high library, with the heavy sand-grey curtains drawn. I gave a computer familiarisation course for their staff. I remember great difficulties and much laughter at the effects of the insert key, and the automatic insertion of carriage returns, and the flow of text from one line to the next, and then even more astonishingly, back if they pressed the delete key. "Look, it was like that. But now is like that. I do not wish it to be like that."

By night we hid on the top floor – with no lights of course. On the days that followed I did some work developing a database of peach varieties for Nino's outfit in Rome – texture, colour, leaf shape, habitat, etc. In the evenings we listened to the news on the roof or twiddled the PC cursors on MS Flight Simulator 4, practising take-offs from Saddam International Airport. But there was a much darker side, worry about Baath party agents in the institution particularly, jeopardising our friends. So finally we took refuge in the colossal, nearly empty research and conference centre Educational Social and Cultural Centre of West Asia (ESCWA), the UN's Middle East headquarters. Here our escape plans centred on putting pressure on the decision makers as the 200 FAO staff melted away to their home countries – fighting robustly for special allowances for this that and the other! Until we were left on our own apart from the FAO Personnel Director, Kevin St Louis, who was a tremendous support. An amateur actor, he loved P.G. Wodehouse, and we enjoyed translating our situations where we were Bertie Wooster and he was the imperturbable and inimitable Jeeves.

By this time elsewhere hostages were feeling much stress, one or two weeping, and one young Italian sitting on the floor, Nino told me, incommunicado with his eyes rolling around distractedly. He was due to get married in Rome in September.

We chose to sleep on banquettes on the vast mezzanine, as if arriving early for a select concert.

Nino phoned Rome and New York talking to officials there to great effect:

"Mr Rawson, you must understand. Our position here is desperate. Our position is **desperate**." Meanwhile I worked on ESCWA's top guys, who were all highly politicised and pro-Iraq. We would enter and sit on the sofa in our latest target ESCWA officer's anteroom before he arrived in the morning. There we would stay, courteously embarrassing, throughout the day and the next until we got an interview and perhaps another level up or across the hierarchy.

Astonishingly, I was occasionally able to get through to the UK by phone in the small hours, joining the Kurdish operator in the FAO exchange. He would route us through to the Baghdad telecoms centre, and we would dial for hours. At the sound of a 44 dialling code or western voice the Iraqi operators would usually just cut the connection, but once in a while I got through. I was very moved one night, sitting with the operator in the small hours, to have him tell me, with misery in his voice: "Why doesn't this fellow President Bush get rid us of this tyrant?"

The UN used its influence to get its people out. Saddam Hussein needed the UN's goodwill, and the last expatriates dwindled. One was held because the expert was a wife, and he was just her husband. Women could not be experts!

Finally just Nino and I were left. Once we nearly got through at the airport, but a second manager called for our passports.

"You see what passports these people carry. Why do you waste our time?"

We slept on sofas in various areas, our favourite spot being the rather fine mezzanine. There was no cooking equipment except for cauldrons etc. for mass meals. But a friend left us his frozen delicacies from Kuwait – all strawberries – when he left, and we cooked in a coffee percolator – excellent for spaghetti! Spaghetti in OXO followed by strawberry. It became a tad boring.

Then on 24th August we got to the administrators' summit, to meet ESCWA's top man, a Jordanian, Tayseer Abdel Jaber. Immensely unpopular at the Institute – he had slumbered visibly throughout the initial presentations the departments had made to him. We pressed him, and he assured me that there was no way he would leave Baghdad until he had got us out. We rejoiced – cautiously.

We sat in Abdel Jaber's office the next morning to make sure the promise stuck. He came in and announced that he was leaving at mid-day and handing us over as refugees.

We got very heated, cited his promise of the night before, and threatened his UN future. It was difficult, I said, for people like him in this situation. FAO in Rome would be watching and judging. He became very angry, as did we. Then a softly-spoken middle-aged Ghanaian came in, one of two deputy UN secretary-generals who had arrived under Security Council Resolution 661 to sort the situation out.

The man had an extraordinary capacity to analyse a situation and pour oil on troubled waters.

"Could you seek shelter with friends?" he asked rhetorically.

No, they might be executed.

Move to a hotel?

No, random snatches were commonplace.

Stay at our homes?

We had none.

So, Abdel Jaber needed to do this, the foreign ministry that, Iraqi Airways the other, a resolution meeting would be held with the following agenda at eleven the next morning.

We watched the spellbinder with hope and more than a tad of scepticism.

"I'll have you out on Wednesday," he said as we joined him in the Hotel Rashid for dinner.

We had several chats with the Ghanaian from New York and Kevin St Louis of FAO over the next three days, notably about the Middle East, and about a paper on its problems by an American who had spent many years as a diplomat in Iran.

Then the Ghanaian called us to a meeting in his suite on the

POST-COLONIAL HOKUM

seventh floor of the Hotel Rashid. There he was with three ambassadors, Harold Walker for the UK, the Italian (for Nino), and the Japanese (for a Japanese who had been trapped in Kuwait and would now be released). He made a speech announcing that the UN had, and always would, secure its staff.

Dujaily's signature was essential for me to be authorised to depart. I met the team in their safe new offices tucked away in the old city. It was a jubilant reunion. Dujaily looked at me, and grinned as he held his pen poised to sign my "Release to Travel".

"For sure of course, Graham, you have failed in your duty to complete our project!"

"For sure of course, Majeed, you have failed in your duty to supply me with the equipment!" (Our Novell networking boards had been rapidly commandeered by the military.)

We were taken to the airport in a flag-waving CD limo, and taken through empty echoing spaces to a special unscheduled flight that was waiting for us. Nino and I were in the two front aisle seats, reserved for us. As we took off we made as if to twiddle the cursors which controlled the aircraft in the MS Flight Simulator 4. She took off safely!

The name of the softly spoken Ghanaian? Kofi Annan, since the immensely successful Secretary General of the UN.

*

I have watched with intense interest the drama of Iraq as it has unfolded in the 20 years since my assignment.

I conclude:

Firstly that people have forgotten what a vile tyranny it was. A million and a half people were killed at Saddam's instigation; he bombed and gassed tens of thousands of his own people; at the start of the second war he was attacking the 500,000 Marsh Arabs, killing them and destroying their way of life. Remember these figures when you consider the deaths in the war. I remember sitting chatting with the night operator (he was occasionally able to connect us through to Congleton about 3am) in the ESCWA HQ. "Why?" he demanded passionately. "Why doesn't Bush destroy this evil man?" To put this into context, consider that you've taken your attractive partner out for the evening to a fashionable restaurant. One of Uday Hussein's henchmen comes in. He sees her, and requests her to sleepover for the night. You both refuse, only at your harshest peril. None of my Iraqi friends took their wives out to dinner!

Secondly, that WMD (weapons of mass destruction) was a mere pretext for the war, a sop particularly to the left-wing politicians. No one, even Saddam's generals, knew whether there were any such weapons, though the generals kept calling for their use during the battles.

The alliance's prime motive was "regime change". An abominable dictatorship had derailed Middle East peace. It needed to be destroyed.

Thirdly, immediately before the invasion people like the UN inspectorate were kidded into trying to institute further delays. But we had a quarter of a million troops in the area waiting to attack. If we had delayed we would have condemned them to fight in the heat of Iraq's summer. Often 47 degrees. Breathe in fast and you blister your gullet. How many deaths from heat stroke might that have caused among our own people? To imagine that Bush and Blair might have kept the army hanging around in the Gulf while the French and Russians played diplomatic games seems incredibly naïf.

Fourthly, the war was an extraordinary success. It was expected to last 125 days, but was over in 25 (Hilary Synott's figures – he was our man in Basra[34]). Imagine the saving of life that resulted.

Fifthly, the peace was an extraordinary disaster; firstly

---

[34] *Bad days in Basra my turbulent time as Britain's Man in Southern Iraq.* Hilary Synnott, IB Tauris & Co, London, 2008.

POST-COLONIAL HOKUM

because Bush kicked over a long-agreed, detailed, and well-prepared plan, and secondly because Blair failed to follow the cornerstone of British colonial policy – "Indirect Rule", and Claire Short, his minister concerned, forbade any attempt to prepare for the peace. We had sufficient "intelligence" to identify key men in the Iraq government who were well-intentioned and able – MI6, the British secret service, visited me twice to get my suggestions. If these key men had been involved, and the process of "Indirect Rule" through well-intentioned members of the Baath party and the Iraq army been followed, I suggest we would have been able to hand over to a fine indigenous government within a couple of years. To outlaw them was incredibly foolish.

Readers may have seen a BBC2 programme about Iraq's Marsh Arabs – the most heartening documentary I've seen in years. How Saddam's destruction of the Euphrates wetlands – possibly the original Garden of Eden – and the fine, self-sufficient culture of the 500,000 robust Marsh Arabs who lived there, has been reversed since the war. He had vast straight canals built to divert the waters away from the wetlands and convert them to desert. And he succeeded.

The programme showed how in the space of five short years since liberation, and against many experts' expectations, the canals have been breached. The reed swamps are regenerating and the wildlife is returning – 40,000 marbled teals for example, like a massive murmuration of starlings. And now the Marsh Arabs are slowly returning to their homelands. This is in great part the achievement of one visionary, Azam al Wash, and his team, working in continuous danger. Recovery of 60,000 square miles from arid desert – unbelievable but true.

If liberal and left-wing Labour politicians had had their way Saddam would still be in power. The wetlands would be desert and an average not of 10 but of 500 Iraqis each day would continue to be barbarously tortured then murdered. That may have been the choice of Iraqis in Birmingham,

Bolton, or Bradford. But for those in Baghdad (and the vast majority elsewhere in Iraq) with whom I worked for the UN in the '90s, Blair's achievement is truly a liberation. A liberation which on democratic and on liberal grounds we should all welcome.

We forget at our peril the abominable history of Saddam's regime, and that he originated three major wars in the tinderbox of the world. His defeat was a triumph for humanity and a full justification for regime change.

To end more positively, peace of a sort has already come to that great country, one of the founts of civilisation, and it may be that we have assisted at the birth pangs of the first Arab democracy.

Or even that it will approach and join the Commonwealth.

The Sudan – The Inshallah Factor

In 1996 I was appointed to the World Bank's South Kordofan Development project in the Southern Sudan. Standard instructions from the Foreign Office were:

PLEASE NOTE:

Southern Sudan is a war zone, and consequently is closed to all travellers.[35] Any attempt to enter this region or travel within it is **extremely dangerous** and definitely not recommended.

*

The Sudan, then the largest country in Africa, was subject to an Anglo-Egyptian Condominium from 1910 to 1955, when it gained independence and immediately embarked on a

---

[35] Getting the necessary permissions from the various authorities required from me 23 passport photos.

socialistic course politically. The period of colonial rule led to an advanced organisation of government in the Arab north of the country, but the remote south, two days away on the wrong side of the Sahara Desert, was neglected. Passionately criticised by the local British DCs, who fought politically for its development.[36]

On the SKADP project, I left Khartoum to cross the Sahara Desert to the project HQ at Kadugli in the Nuba Mountains in Southern Sudan on 4th August 1996. A month later, my wife received a telex from the SKADP HQ in Khartoum:

"Mr Tottle sends greetings to all his family, and Birthday wishes to his second son, Bartholomew."

I have no second son Bartholomew. Bartholomew was our first dog, a fine black and white Labramation.

*

This section tries to fill in what happened during that lost month of my life. I still find the writing stressful and depressing. Too many unanswered questions:

Was I deliberately drugged or otherwise impaired by people in Kordofan to safeguard their $40 million World Bank project against adverse reports by an interfering expat?

Was I the focus of a southerners' rebellion?

Was there a religious component, between the southern Christians and pagans and the northern Muslims?

---

[36] Typical of these remote and doughty administrators was Gus Fergusson, whom I knew later in Kigezi as Resettlement Officer. The truck operator who contracted with him to bring through the government mail once a month (Jeremy Paxman Please note – this man was not an automaton at the electronic whim of clerks in Whitehall) failed to do so. Fergusson had the bridge taken out, trapping the truck on the wrong side, until the service was agreed to be resumed.

Or was I just the victim of an overstressed imagination pushed over the limit by the harshness of the environment, the violence of life in the war zone, and the competitive stresses within the project?

My project, SKADP (South Kordofan Agricultural Development Project), was situated in the Nuba Mountains, in this area, the war zone (still) south of the desert. The war had been in constant ebb and flow for thirty years, the Brits having given the Sudan independence in 1955, a confrontation between the socialist Arab regime and culture in the north and the Nilotic and Nilo-hamitic Bantu tribes in the south. A confrontation fomented by religious differences, between Islam in the North and Paganism – spirit worship – and Christianity in the south. The Sudanese had (and have as the crises in neighbouring Darfur show) no wish to have interfering westerners in those parts. But they needed the SKADP money, $40 million, desperately, and World Bank HQ demanded independent monitoring and evaluation to ensure their funds were being well-spent. The Bank was dissatisfied to put it mildly, and the warlords, who ran Kordofan and similar parts, refused even to grant the Bank officials access to check what was going on. So, we three Brits had been brought in to carry this out:

One (Oliver) the Management Engineer, looking at transport and equipment (tractors were being blown up by mines, and Land Rovers were being commandeered and converted into war vehicles with heavy machine guns mounted on tripods in the body).

One (Tom Davies) Team Leader, a General Agriculturalist looking at overall project management, and one, myself, Head of the Information Systems Unit, to define and secure "M&E", as the jargon has it – Monitoring and Evaluation of planning, progress, and resources across all the project's disciplines. The project's prime target was agriculture, but water conservation, crop storage facilities, factory processing facilities, transport and infrastructure improvement were all included.

POST-COLONIAL HOKUM

To convey the colossal difficulties which the project endured: there was no postal/telecoms system to Kordofan; water was short, the drinking water seeping down from near a public latrine; there were no local supplies of diesel, so our fuel had to be transported across 1,300 miles of deeply rutted desert tracks from the Red Sea coast in our five big eight-wheel tankers. Kordofan in 1992 was more backward than most African countries were in 1930.[37] Our project was to cover 138,000 square miles, twice the area of the UK, of savannah, desert, and mountains, for polyglot peoples ranging through nomad pastoralists, transhumant pastoralists (the Nuer), to livestock (camels, cattle, chickens, sheep, goats) and to some "sedentary" agriculture, cultivating primarily sorghum, the local cereal crop and mangoes. The Project Proposal is a fascinating document. A strictly factual, matter-of-fact, definition of an impossible objective. And all this to be achieved with a vicious irreconcilable civil war in progress.

My friend Curtis Pastik's team of 11, doing a Land Utilisation Project[38], were allowed out to selected areas (we were confined to the 5km main road from Kadugli to the

---

[37] One morning I was invited in for coffee (arab-style) as I passed, by a very large and friendly shopkeeper. He and his friend harked back to a certain Mr. Jones, their teacher in the forties, whom they still revered fifty years on. One recited, accurately, Wordsworth's Daffodils:
"Beside the lake beneath the trees.
 Fluttering and dancing in the breeze."
[38] Curtis held that global warming was a figment of the imagination of ambitious climatologists, but he was instructed to gain any relevant climate data. To his surprise, firstly the recording system set up by the imperialist Brits in 1930 had still been carried out over half a century, and secondly it confirmed, for a great swathe of Africa across the Sahara, that warming was occurring just as predicted. He included in the Land Utilisation plan a provision for research into new crops – a cultivar of finger millet, I think, - to replace the sorghum beloved by the locals. Curtis went on to become head in the UN High Commission for Refugees in Rwanda

Project HQ) and came back with useful pointers. Most worrying were the occasional big open trucks crowded up and wailing with people who seemed to overnight at transit camps out in the savannah en route north. We were told they were refugees. We suspected they were Bantu slaves en route to Arabia, as had been the practice a century earlier until blocked by the Brits in 1900. Two years later, in 1992, a detailed report in the *Observer* showed we were right. The Pastik team's most fascinating discovery was that the remains still existed of tanks (dams) built by the engineers of the Meroitic kingdom in the 5th century AD, and disused and abandoned for 1,200 years. Their rehabilitation was built into the Water Development plan on which I was working. Atif Hassan worked with me, and helped defuse one row. For water monitoring the scientists clearly needed rain gauges. These had been requisitioned and paid for a year earlier, but had still not arrived. So, the Chief Water Engineer insisted, rainfall recording could not take place. I went down to the town and got some glass bottles and plastic funnels and showed that you could split the glass horizontally by filling it to the appropriate mark with oil, then plunging in a red hot poker. Put a simple funnel on top, mark off the level on the sides, and there is your gauge. He was furious and left in a huff. They were highly trained professionals. His people were not prepared to accept Mickey-Mouse solutions. Atif went away and smoothed things down. I relaxed – the gauges weren't pivotal to the plan, which was to do with dam repair and canal/aqueduct construction.

I had noticed an "Inception Report" by Oliver on the files, summarising the position on his engineering project when he arrived. Copied to Masdar and, crucially, to the World Bank. This seemed a way of getting through to the PMU management, so I drafted my own, "Inception Report" and included an accurate but fairly damning summary of progress on the project to date – giving much of the background I'd given informally for the World Bank review. In casual discussions among expats I'd suggested a major problem in the Sudan was "The Inshallah Factor". Inshallah is the Arabic and Islamic word for "God willing". And their God, as described brilliantly in the article I'd given to Kofi Annan, is a God who is incalculably powerful and remote, symbolised by the fierce heat, blinding sun, and the harshness of the desert environment. Good intentions signify nothing if they do not suit His irresistible and inscrutable will.

This word, "Inshallah", came into any discussion on progress and plans, as it does in many Arab countries. To me it conveyed a lack of confidence and determination which, I thought, contributed greatly to project problems. No one would rely on anything happening, hence the mentality of the Soukh, the market. Trust no one and make your bargain while you can. Yesterday's friend may well be tomorrow's enemy. But burnt into my experience was that our ICL computer operating systems could never have been created if this attitude had prevailed. In ICL you stated you dependencies on others, e.g. for a disc file driver to such and such a specification and date. They signed it off as a commitment, and woe betide them if they failed to meet it. And woe betide you if, when it was provided, you didn't immediately fall on it and use it. Milestones and Dependencies, fundamental to sound management.

That was the attitude needed for this project. Of course agriculturalists would respond that agriculture was "not like that". Too many imponderable variables – climate, disease, cultivations, planting materials, supplies, labour, credit, marketing and so on and so on. Even so, look at the success of the Malaysians in RISDA, and of the new smallholder tea and coffee organisations in East and Central Africa, where SCAPA was doing its stuff, and where long-established estates in Sri Lanka were being outperformed.

I terminated my report urging the need for attitudes to change, and for us to be aware of the **"Inshallah Factor"** as a source of uncertainty. Well knowing this phrase might for religious reasons give offence to Muslims and create thereby attention and action. Alison typed it and I sent it off as a "draft for discussion" to the Sheikh, to Masdar, but also to senior people in the project and key contacts to provoke a response.

The Sheikh called me in:

"Graham, this has been seen by many people, and has given offence."

"But it is a serious problem."

"Maybe so. But it has given offence."

Masdar in the UK were never to receive their copy.

In Khartoum, I left word quietly for the Sheikh that I was going to attend his new monthly meeting at Kadugli in two days' time, as he had firmly agreed with Tom Davies before he left for the UK. I would test things out.

Would the meeting be held? I wondered. Would he be there or not? This was the acid test of their commitment. Exciting stuff!

Atif told me that seventeen people had been killed in Kadugli in a battle the week before – a matter too trivial to get into the national press. He suggested we delayed our departure – but this would negative the acid test. So I set off with him for the South. Black thunderheads spouting blinding rainstorms hit us en route, and we were forced to overnight in a thatched hut miles from anywhere. The next morning, a hundred grinding miles further on, the main bridge had been swept away. We detoured via the desert and got bogged down to the axles in the saturated sand. We were eventually dragged out by a tractor in blazing sunshine, and made a hazardous fording of the offending river. It was an astonishing experience. They place men on the line of the shallowest water, just below shoulder depth, and you go full belt in the jeep, zigzagging from one man to the next. Full belt because the resultant bow wave round the bonnet keeps the engine's fan clear of the water even though it's actually below water level. Rather as a bow wave builds up round the bow of a boat and leaves a trough in the water behind it. Slow down and the effect dies... and so does your engine.

Towards nightfall we reached the transition between desert and the savannah, only forty miles to go, when we encountered a convoy of SKADP vehicles coming in the opposite direction. I was greeted courteously, but peripherally. The project team walked around on the road grasping each other by hands and slapping the forearms, hilariously amused about something. Then they all turned around, and followed us towards Kadugli.

We were stopped at an army road block in the savannah and scrub ten miles on. A very educated and courteous young captain came to see me. There was an "operation" in progress, and we must camp in his perimeter for the night. He, Atif told me, was all right – one of "us", and could be trusted.

We pulled off the road at an encampment and I tried to settle down for the night, visited by one or two of the team, who found my low-slung mosquito net hilariously funny. There was little sign of Atif, but I guess he was renewing friendship with others in the team. I felt laughed at, annoyed, isolated.

Then came an episode which was to colour my future for many years. I slept fitfully, and at about five – pitch dark in the tropics – got up and started to stroll round the area. Suddenly I looked around and found I couldn't identify my hut. Lost. But there was a faint glow as of a fire in one direction. I wandered slowly towards it. I came up to a grass hut, or rather open shelter, and there by the side of a glowing smouldering fire were an old man and his wife. I felt a sudden sense of immense peace, of a permanent significance in this moment. Quite uncanny. I greeted them as usual:

"Salaam aleikum."

"Aleikum salaam!"

"Alhamdulillah."

"Alhamdulillah."

I stood for a long moment, and they looked at me. Then I drifted away, and sat down on the sand to wait for dawn.

When it came, Atif came up and greeted me, smiling. But he seemed thunderously annoyed when I described my meeting with the old people.

We moved off to have breakfast along the road. Small pieces of liver simmered in a sauce, and eaten with your hands from a communal tureen. Not appetising when eaten for the third day in succession!

I felt a sort of worried detachment, and after we reached the project, sat at a desk outside on the sand for a while, then went to the compound five miles away.

When I'd settled in there was a sudden burst of heavy machine gun fire from the barracks close by. I dived to the floor, recalling the experience of some friends in a similar situation in Kampala under Idi Amin. Forget your dignity, concentrate on surviving!

Like on the foredeck of a yacht in a gale – crouch down and hang on and crawl around – much more effective than standing in dignity as the rise of a wave hurls you over the side!

The firing went on desultorily for maybe a quarter of an hour. Then there was quiet. I settled down then heard stealthy noises outside. I flung the door open, and there was a fit, heavyset young army officer with my cook. I flung a punch at him, thinking he was persecuting the little cook. He parried it with ease, smiling as he did so, and grabbed me. I was taken down to stand at an office window I was to get to know later, and interrogated. All I would give was my name and affiliation – as in "name rank and number" one was told to give in the army if captured. Nothing else.

The next incident I recall was sitting at a long table in the open, evening time, with about six officials interrogating me, and, I thought, numerous people behind me. In the open before a long, low building, and with a low hedge behind me. I felt that I was under deep threat, refused to answer many questions, then suddenly flung myself upwards, flinging my arms outwards, and letting out a colossal shout. *They might well kill me*, I thought, *but rumours might survive for Philip, my son, to track down in years to come*. Why my son and not my three daughters, you may wonder! In extremis, the atavistic instincts survive, however liberal and enlightened you may think you are. The son's the one to seek his dad!

I was bundled on a stretcher and trundled to a hospital ward. There I was awakened in the night by the sound of many people coming past. Just visible in the light from dim oil lamps. A bit like being the corpse with mourners filing past. An educated voice said: "He talked to them in their own tongue, they say. Just like one of them."

"Nonsense."

"That's what they say."

I was kept in hospital, an armed guard with a Kalashnikov in the corner of the ward, and Atif was sent to Khartoum.

Two further incidents stand out. In the first I was talking to three of the team, led by the Agricultural Advisor.

"Can we now start the Lotus (spreadsheet) course?" I asked.

"No. We have not finished you yet," was the grinding, frightening answer.

And another day, I was taken to the Land Rover with my kit to stand in front of them on a grassy patch.

"Now we will say goodbye to you," the advisor said in a hostile tone. Then he turned triumphantly to the others: "First Oliver," he said, "then Davies. And now Tottle." They laughed. They'd got rid of the World Bank Brits. We roared off down the rough track northwards, perhaps, I think, to get past hostile road blocks, until we reached the provincial boundary. Then more sedately to El Obeid, halfway across the desert, for the night. I spent much of it turning the room's light on and off – dit, dit, dit – dah, dah, dah – dit, dit, dit. The Morse code for S.O.S., "Save our Souls". But no one came! Then on across the desert to Khartoum.

My wife had realised the telex about my son "Bartholomew" and the non-existent birthday was a plea for help, that something strange was up. She got onto Masdar and set in train actions which had eventually had me moved back across the desert, affected by acute psychosis, to hospital in Khartoum. Thence they removed me to the American embassy (I apparently fought to get away) and there a formidable doctor fixed electrodes around my head and torso, and for some time shouted in my face imprecations which I didn't understand. After he was satisfied with whatever he was doing, he relaxed and put me in a cot in his office. The next morning I was taken by a British psychiatric nurse to the airport and hustled across a waiting zone towards a plane. "This is a very ripe fruit cake indeed," I overheard him saying. He then had to take me off the first plane home because I was too violent, and keep me in the US security compound till the next. Thence I was put in the splendid cavernous Parkside mental hospital in Macclesfield, near my home. There it took a month's gentle treatment, and the healing effects of its lovely green parkland, to bring me back to partial sanity.

*

A failure of the colonial system's successor, and of the scramble for Africa in the 1890s which had invented this impossible country – now, in 2012, divided into two, but still at war.

Chapter 18

Transport

Transport is obviously fundamental to the imperial and Commonwealth links. I'll just cover some aspects I've got to know personally on rail, sea, and sky.

Firstly, sea. The picture shows the parade of ships celebrating the opening of the Suez Canal. It's just possible that my great-great grandfather was skippering one of them, though most of the ancestors were sealing and whaling in the west Pacific.

Graphics from "The story of the P&O".

The global picture as regards the most prominent of the great shipping lines, the P&O – Peninsular and Oriental – in the 1950s is shown in their diagram below.

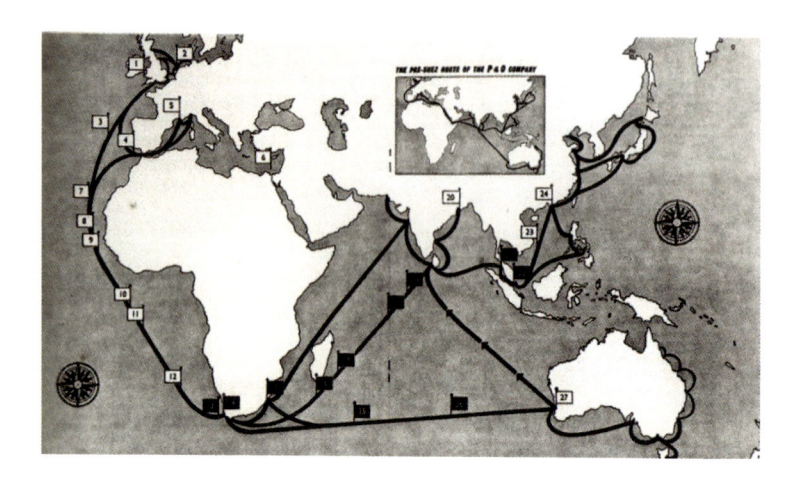

They were a great organisation, but there were other British and Commonwealth competitors across from Australia to the Americas. My father, as one of their skippers, had a dramatic collision with an Australian freighter at night in Sydney harbour in 1951. He just managed to beach his ship as she was sinking.

Graphic from Captain Thomas Harpham Bews Tottle.

She was then part of the Asiatic Steam Navigation Company's fleet, eventually to join the P&O, and to disappear from the seas in the 1980s except as cruise liners.

Air Transport

I can't resist showing some front runners, even though in one case, the Sunderland flying boat, my link is tenuous. All of them were designed with the Commonwealth requirements at heart.

Short Sunderland Flying Boats

Hugh Fraser, my first DC in Uganda, used to go and return from leave in this wonderful aircraft, flying up the Nile to Lake Victoria from Alexandria in 700-mile skips.

Quote from the French site "Metalique":

The Short Sunderland flying boat was developed for communication around the empire, and was one of the mainstays of Coastal Command during WW2 and he was one of the longest serving military aircraft of its era, with an RAF career from 1938 until 1959. They served also in the Royal Canadian Air Force and the Royal New Zealand Air Force. In the early 1930s, competition in development of long-range flying boats for intercontinental passenger service was becoming increasingly intense and Great Britain had nothing to match the new American Sikorsky flying boats In 1934, the British postmaster general declared that all first-class Royal Mail sent overseas was to travel by air, effectively establishing a subsidy for the development of intercontinental air transportation. So British Imperial Airways announced a competition for an order for 28 flying boats, each weighing 16.4 tonnes (18 tons) and having a range of 1,130 kilometres (700 miles) with a capacity of 24 passengers Early in 1934 Imperial had asked Shorts to work on a design for an updated version of the Kent-type flying boat, with a range of 800 miles, 24 passengers and 1.5 tons of mail. Oswald Short, began a crash program with at the head of the design team Arthur Gouge. The design produced, the Short "S.23", was a clean and elegant aircraft, with a wingspan of 35 meters a length of 27 meters, an empty weight of 10.9 tons and a loaded weight of 18.4 tons. The S.23 was powered by four Bristol Pegasus air-cooled radial engines, each providing 686 kW (920 HP). Cruise speed was 265 KPH (165 MPH), and maximum speed was 320 KPH. The S.23 featured a new hull design and a new flap scheme to reduce landing speed and run. The big flying boat had two decks: an upper deck for the flight crew and mail, and a lower deck with luxury passenger accommodations.

Graphic from the French site "Metalique".

The first S.23, named *CANOPUS*, made its first flight on July 4th 1936 and she was the first of a series of Shorts flying boats for commercial service, collectively known as the "Empire" boats. A total of 41 S.23s were built, all with names beginning with the letter "C", and so they were also referred to as the "C-class" boats.

*

The first flying boat service out to Hong Kong met with two big problems. One big problem was the crystal clear lagoons in the Arabian Gulf used for landing and taking off. In calm weather the pilots couldn't see the surface to land on it. But they had to – no alternatives in those parts. So there were numerous thundering bashes as they hit the surface. The answer was ping-pong balls. They used to make two passes over the lagoon. The first time they opened sacks of ping pong balls, which went floating down. They spread out on the surface so at the second circuit the pilot could see it and land safely.

Another was the vicious hostility of the tribes in the Gulf area – you might suffer an agonising death after torture if you had to make an emergency landing. The answer was the "ball chitty", a document in Arabic and English, sewn into your shorts. It assured the reader of a substantial reward in Maria Theresa dollars if the wearer was returned to base intact.

Graphic from "Century of Flight".

A BBC series in 2012 alleged mistakenly and repeatedly that "Pan American Airways kick-started the era of jet travel".

In fact the era was kick-started in 1949, eight years before the US Boeing 707, a converted US air force tanker, was first introduced by Pan Am. Kick-started by the British de Havilland Comet, perhaps the loveliest jet liner ever. It carried 28,000 passengers in its first year, had orders for fifty more, and it seemed likely it would dominate commercial aviation for the next forty years. The editor of *American Aviation Magazine* said, "Whether we like it or not, the British are giving the U.S. a drubbing in jet transport."

I remember enjoying an early flight to Uganda, soaring quietly and swiftly way above the weather which gave piston-engined planes a slow bumpy and uncomfortable ride.

De Havilland's success was a result of imagination and inventiveness. And the Comet's subsequent tragedy resulted from another British trait, what in International Computers we used to call "the NIH syndrome" – Not Invented Here. De Havilland resolved to power their revolutionary airframe with their in-house engine rather than the more powerful products of their competitors, Bristol or Rolls Royce. This colossal error meant that the fuselage and wings had to be built with wafer-thin thickness. After an immensely successful first year there were four fatal crashes. On the fourth, a BOAC Comet departing from Rome climbed to 26,000 feet, en route to its assigned altitude of 36,000 feet. Captain Alan Gibson began to radio a message to another BOAC plane behind him. "Did you get my…"

Silence.

Seconds later, fishermen near the island of Elba saw the remains of the Comet plunge into the sea and the planes were grounded. Tank testing followed, the results made available to all the industry, showing that this resulted from metal fatigue weakness and from the designers' wish not to give it the appearance of a ship, and so using square portholes. From the square corners stretched cracks, causing explosions at high altitudes. A great friend of mine was Airport Manager, BOAC (now BA) Colombo. He used to dread the arrival of a Comet in the rainy season – spray from the wheels on landing peppered the ailerons with holes, and the passengers had to be moved to hotels while a new set of ailerons was flown out.

It was a disaster, but a disaster arising from courage and inventiveness. And showing the Brits' leadership; leadership not by the Irish, not by the English, not by the Welsh, not by the Scots, but by that splendid amalgam, the British, who've been in the vanguard for five centuries. Witness many of the last century's greatest innovations, usually unsung, e.g. in computing, pharmaceuticals, entertainment, finance, urban design, architecture. I remember the *Guardian* whingeing in 1968: "Sadly all the future software innovations will come from Germany and Japan." Forty years down the track, and we're still waiting for them!

Vickers VC10

On the way home from a management research assignment with the Kenyan Ministry of Co-operatives in 1978, ICL directed me to do a week's research with their computer people in Ghana into their cocoa industry. It was a fascinating experience. The Kenyans controlled all coffee production in strictness and in depth, with ever-increasing success. But in Ghana, after independence, Kwame Nkrumah milked the smallholder cocoa producers beyond all reason, enabling him to keep his supporters in the big cities on side with cheap food etc. As a result the smallholders smuggled their produce across the borders, much as did their counterparts in Uganda. Farms in the border area in Kenya were smashing world records for coffee production per hectare as smuggled coffee flooded in! Nkrumah then bolstered his position by moving favoured regiments of the army to the borders to control – and milk –

the smuggling operation. As a result Ghana's supremacy in the world market for cocoa collapsed. Kofi Annan, when UN Secretary General, rightly said that Africa has been ill-served by many of its rulers.

How does this relate to the VC10? I joined it, a lovely aircraft, on the tarmac at Accra. They used in early days to say the Brits bury their engines in the wings – the Comet – the French put them in the tail, where they belong, while the Yanks bury them in the ground – the Boeing 107! The VC10 had four engines placed just like the French Caravelles, just forward of the tail. This targeted the massive Commonwealth demand for aircraft which could operate from the short runways of that time.

I settled in, we moved along the tarmac, and then she took off after a strikingly short run at an unbelievably steep angle. And in virtual silence since the engines were thrusting us from behind.

A classic piece of brilliant design, fouled up, as with the Blue Streak in space rocketry and with ICL in computing, by government short termism and incompetence. They should have forced British Airways to honour their commitments (they reneged) to buy the VC10. They didn't. It matters who runs the airlines. But it matters massively who innovates and designs at the leading edge of technology. British seed corn was squandered by the Conservatives – in the pockets of the bankers and city – and Labour – in the pockets of the unions.

Graphic from BAE Systems.

Britten-Norman Trislander. Graphic from Deutsch Wikipedia.

In 1990 I had a challenging and enjoyable assignment for installation and training for SCAMPA (described in Chapter 9) in Malawi for the tea authority (EEC).

Most of our work was done close to the old capital, Blantyre, but I went at the request of the Commonwealth Development Corporation (CDC) to Mzuzu in the remote north. It was a fine taste of the capacity of the aircraft industry's planes way out in the sticks.

We took off from Blantyre and flew east to the great lake, Malawi. Then flew north by line of sight, following the lake shore, eventually over clouds, so that it was impossible to pick out the airport. The pilot circled around till he found a gap in the clouds, dropped down to the lake, then turned inland when he found and followed the main road to Mzuzu. Then we landed, and while we waited for the CDC – in a fine Range Rover, then new to the world – the refuelling of the plane started. A worker climbed a ladder and up on top of the plane, opened the fuel tap, and proceeded to refuel. He held a large umbrella over the fuel hose even though he was in blazing sun and a cloudless sky. I guess it was standard procedure, because rainwater in the fuel tank would be disastrous. The Trislander was a workhorse for these remote environments.

Since this book is concerned with the Commonwealth I should expand a little on the great history of the CDC. They were trailblazers for some of the most advanced and successful development projects, often piloting or leading on to major World Bank activities for example. They were good and they knew it, and this meeting was, for me, typical of their attitudes. The bluff, bronzed, cheerful leader who met us in his top of the range, gleaming new Range Rover gave us lunch. Then listened with condescension to the ideas we wanted to explore. Then made it clear that if there was any future in them, the CDC had brilliant computing people back at base who would have done it all already! The CDC has now been mistakenly re-engineered into a straightforward commercially minded outfit – a loss to the world of international development.

Chapter 19

Mining

In the general debate about the Kenyan Hola atrocities and Mau Mau on 18th July 2012, the words "extraction" and "exploitation" kept recurring, as they do frequently in debates about the Empire.

In 40 years I have come across very many mines across various Commonwealth countries, and I'd like to explore how far the accusations apply.

On one night in the rest house on Lake Mutanda I was joined by the government geologist. A middle-aged man, very athletic and at degree level long qualified in his discipline. His enthusiasm for his day's work was intense and infectious. He had discovered that the whole 600-foot high and 10-mile wide hill or small mountain below which we stood had been rolled over 180 degrees like a rounders bat at some unknown geological time, with immensely exciting effects, not just in terms of the mineral resources revealed but part of this wonderful country and our wonderful planet. This was man discovering for the first time how these parts had been built.

Kigezi was full of such features, and one of the most interesting concerned Kikkides, a dark-haired, brown-complexioned Cypriot peasant, lean face carved as if of mahogany, who had travelled south soon after WW2. All Kikkides knew about geology was that a precious metal was heavier than your standard stone. He came down through Ethiopia, looking around, and set up a tent near Kisoro. After discussion with the Muruka chief he took on some local young men, instructing them to bring him rocks which were especially heavy and tell him where they came from. One day one searcher came in with a block of black, heavy, shining stuff. Kikkides' eyes glinted. Perhaps he had hit the jackpot. He put the rock in a knapsack, got on the bus over the mountains to Kampala, took his rock to the geological research laboratories and asked them to assess it. He stayed a couple of days in Kampala, short of money, and then got the result. The rock was wolfram.[39] He registered a mineral claim to mine the hill concerned, and got a loan for the machinery and labour to develop it. When I visited the mine on an inspection some years down the line, the hill was carved into massive steps from top to bottom, each step being about 20 feet wide and 20 feet high. It was a striking construct. On a hill opposite was Kikkides' large house and garden, and he was a friendly easy-going millionaire. The wolfram was a semi-precious rock, essential in the construction of military aircraft (and later space rockets) and he had hit the crest of the massive wave of demand at the beginning of the Korean War. He showed initiative and imagination and, as they say, he had run with the ball. The Mines Department of the Protectorate Government, represented in Western Province by a Canadian, Les Job (who sold me a very dodgy four-litre Plymouth Station wagon!), had carried out all the procedures required to ensure that extraction was appropriately managed, that the labour rates were being met.

How far was this exploitation? I suggest not at all. Kikkides created employment, wealth for the country, and the

---

[39] From Wikipedia: It has the highest melting point of all the non-alloyed metals and the second highest of all the elements after carbon. Also remarkable is its high density of 19.3 times that of water, comparable to that of uranium and gold, and much higher (about 1.7 times) than that of lead. Tungsten with minor amounts of impurities is often brittle and hard, making it difficult to work. However, very pure tungsten, though still hard, is more ductile, and can be cut with a hard-steel hacksaw.

government revenues were collected.

This applies equally to various other mines in Kigezi, notably to one set up by a Norwegian named Spiropoulos.

One of my functions as ADC 4 was a weekly trip down to the Kigezi Recruitment Agency run by an easy-going guy, Len Scard. They recruited workers for the Kilembe copper mines, the biggest mining operation in Uganda – big enough to warrant 100 or so miles of railway – and for various other large firms. I went down to read out the terms and conditions of employment to all the young men were being recruited that week, and these were translated for them by the agency's interpreter. The whole thing seemed immensely cheerful, simple, and above board and the young men would be employed for between three and six months on contract. They were generally excited, and those with experience were joshing those who were newcomers. Is that exploitation or is it a normal and well understood employment process? Is this strictly overseen procedure not vastly more protective of labour recruitment than that which pertains worldwide? Of the other mining applications with which I came into contact in forty years, the most notable were the copper mining operations round Ndola in Zambia, source of most of the country's wealth, and the tin mines in Malaysia equally vital to the economy. These also seemed to be well run on, following the procedures originally set up by the Brits before independence. Though pollution of the water courses was a real problem, being tackled by the Malaysian government.

These are further instances of the importance of handing down tried and tested institutions and procedures across the Commonwealth. Is this exploitation, as the critics suggest?

Chapter 20

Conclusion

I hope the book has interested and pleased you, and a further version covering other topics and countries is targeted on Easter 2016. It will include work in Bangladesh, Ghana, Malawi, Nigeria, Sri Lanka, Zimbabwe and Zambia, with diversions outside to the US, China, and North Korea.

Topics: land, credit, survey, water, sustainability, IT, engineering, ILO, FAO, DFID, EU.

*

I'd like now to draw the threads together by painting two snapshots, one of a single, isolated colonial officer's activity in the remotest Sudan in 1902, and the other from my final involvement for DIFID and the European Union in the Banana War in 1990.

On 15/10/2012 the postmodernist "Amdram" historian, Professor David Reynolds, concluded his pieces on BBC4 TV by saying, "The British Empire was just a con trick."

As Churchill might have said, some con... some trick!

Without the Empire and Commonwealth of nations it seems unlikely that the 20th century's victories over totalitarianism, Nazism, and Stalinism, would have come to pass. Reynolds lacked the nous to comprehend the extraordinary transformation which occurred in just sixty or so years between primitive societies like Uganda – to quote Thomas Hobbes from the 17th century, "the life of man poor, brutish and short" – and modern, happy, civilisation in 1963.

I'd like to end with two snapshots of this transformation to illustrate the point. One from the remotest Southern Sudan in 1902, when sleeping sickness was decimating the population, and the other from the West Indies in 1990, when they and the Brits – Commonwealth members working in happy conjunction – were exploring the future, exploring how advancing technology can benefit immensely the prosperity and humanity, of the planet. For example, particularly in the Windies, the smallholder farmers (Schumacher's *Small is Beautiful*).[40]

Snapshot 1:

First days. Sleeping sickness, or trypanosomiasis, is carried by the tsetse fly much as malaria is carried by the anopheles mosquito, and still kills 50,000 people a year. Its worst phase occurs when the parasite attacks the nerves and brain, breaking up the sleep/wake cycle and leading inevitably to coma and death. In 1902 sleeping sickness was killing thousands in East and Central Africa, and one area of Uganda was completely emptied of people by the disease. The same problem was occurring in the southern Sudan, and one man who had been appointed District Commissioner of an area took it by the throat. The area was populated by various clans who were allegedly ungovernable, frequently mutually hostile and often murderous and viciously in conflict. Evans Prichard, the social anthropologist whom we met earlier, describes their strange, yet quite effective, system of justice. If you murdered a man your crime had to be punished with death or with the equivalent in cattle, similarly to the bride price. A procedure similar to the wergild in Saxon times in the UK.

---

[40]Erwin Schumacher, *Small is Beautiful – a study of economics as if people mattered* – the great economist who originated integrated thinking about environmentalism in the 60s and 70s.

This challenging social environment was made even more violent when sleeping sickness came. Smith knew a means of fairly effective containment, notably clearing of bush the banks around the streams and rivers where the fly flourished. By dint of personality and prestige he persuaded the chiefs to take action, and held courts to punish offenders. The disease was largely eliminated, and the fragile authority of the Anglo-Egyptian condominium was greatly strengthened. As elsewhere, the results in terms of human happiness are largely ignored by the critics, and must have been massive.

Snapshot 2:

Recent history. I've been involved in many exciting projects arising from the Empire and Commonwealth. For example, the Sudan Gezira Board, where a British innovator in 1904 noted that there was a shallow 3° slope in the vast area concerned, and asked himself, "How about irrigated wheat or cotton, using the slightly sloping plain (of dense, leak-free clay) to move the water around through canals?" The results for the country and for British textile industry were dramatic – 2,500 miles of canals and ditches, one of the largest irrigation schemes in the world. Was this colonialist exploitation?

But the West Indian banana industry is one on which I would like to conclude.

As background, the topic is "Imperial preference". I remember my teenage nieces condemning it as we chatted in the early 70s. Shocking exploitation, she said. The fact that I had served in the Colonial Service and knew the detail counted for nothing. Their teacher had told them! That was the attitude which gradually came to permeate British thinking about the Empire and Commonwealth.

The same view was put by Jeremy Paxman sneeringly:

"This was a trading doctrine of Imperial Preference whereby the country which had sermonised the world on the life-giving virtues of free trade introduced tariffs on goods from countries which had the misfortune not to belong to the Empire."[41] Never mind about our long cultural, economic, scientific, democratic, institutional links.

For him and his like,[42] the Empire was to be derided, and the Commonwealth a sham invented to disguise imperial decline.

Let's now look at one case of the Imperial preference, arising from the vital smallholder banana industry which Britain and the West Indies had created and cherished.

In 1998 Nick Freeland, a Director of the consultancy Masdar, phoned me from Thailand. Might I be interested in an assignment in the West Indies in St Vincent?[43] I jumped at the idea. I flew into St Lucia, a mountainous, beautiful isle, favourite among honeymooners. I was picked up from the

---

[41] *Empire*, p. 247, Jeremy Paxman, Penguin Books.

[42] I remember Paxman and Palin guffawing rather repellently at the imperial scenario in his TV series. Ian Hislop has recently reviewed the "stiff upper lip", an emotional attitude which has served us well for centuries and which he hopes will return after our weep-prone present. Not just a Victorian invention – consider Paget, later Marquess of Anglesey, at the battle of Waterloo. Paget, at the head of the cavalry, was desperately wounded by grapeshot in a charge during the battle. "By God, sir," he told Wellington as they rode after the French, "I've lost my thigh."
"By God, sir," answered the Duke. "So you have," and rode firmly onward. Long, as Hislop's interviewee, an MP, suggested, long may the stiff lip persist.

[43] Database design and implementation for Management Information System, for all operations, targetting on ORACLE under Netware. I was to be lead analyst in a system which covers all the functions listed since they want to integrate all their main functions, Input Supply, Production , Manufacture, Marketing, Accounting and Extension.

airport and driven to the Geest House. Geest, I remembered, were the Dutch firm who set up the early "banana boat" system and ran all the six related ships between the islands and Britain and Holland The "Geest House" was an enchanting fairy-tale complex of airy rooms spaced in a demi-semicircle round a sprawling marble patio, looking through a border of jungle and palms onto a beach and the harbour, with a glimpse between cliffs of the ocean. Designed for himself by the original Meneer Geest, a creative Dutch multi-millionaire of taste and imagination.

The Windward Islands Headquarters of the EU support project covered all the islands – self-governing but often working and playing international cricket in concert. This HQ was central to what has become known as the "Banana War" – featured in three pages by Lucy Siegle of a 1998 edition of *The Observer*. The war is a struggle between the US and the EU. The EU want to maintain a form of the "imperial preference" which the West Indian smallholders used to enjoy under the British Empire and Commonwealth in competing with massive US mechanised corporations like Dole and Chiqita on the South American mainland. I spent two days absorbing their views of activities and priorities, then flew on to St Vincent.

St Vincent, like most of the other Windwards, but on a vaster vertical scale, is a towering volcanic island, rising straight out of the deep Atlantic. It's jungle and banana-girt on the lower slopes, tropical rain forest among the high crags. The volcano, La Souffriere, is occasionally live. "Found" by Columbus on his third voyage, "Windward" because they are the islands the Europeans first reached, to windward of the rest. Not at all popular with tourists, for it has only one tiny strip of yellow tourist-friendly sand and much dark, coarse volcanic sand fringing many precipitous coves. So deep you can't anchor yachts, and they have to use shore lines to palm trees from one side of a cove to another. At substantial rental to the tree-owners!

Graphic from photo by author.

Its one harbour is dominated by Young Island. It's a pinnacle of rock atop which six British marines and a gun once held the French blockaded for several months. There you feel as if you are in a naval yarn of the 1790s by the incomparable Patrick O'Brian. The French and Brits fought over St Vincent for two centuries, in which the island changed hands 14 times. Escaped slave communities lived up in the peaks and raided both sides effectively and impartially. The tropical semi-paradise is the scene of an ICL IT drama, because IT is one of the keys in the economic struggle between the independent, impoverished smallholders of the islands, and the powerful, mechanised, US-owned estates, Chiquita and Dole, on the South American mainland – the prize being the banana slots in European householders' pantries. The key issue is whether the smallholders, with only up to 3 acres of hillside apiece, can excel in quality the produce of the big South American estates despite the estates' great advantages of flat land (the

Vincentians have to cultivate on slopes as steep as the flanks of the English downs), size, mechanisation, capital, and large-scale production.

I flew in and settled into one of three hotels in Umbrella Bay by Young Island Cut, the channel between Young Island and the mainland. Exquisitely beautiful. Then I went into Kingstown to work. SVBGA, the St Vincent Banana Grower's Association. It was in sombre, dark, green, two-storey offices in the south of the town, in a vast factory and shipping areas dominating the port, and also in dispersed extension and processing centres under the mountains among the growers. Bananas were by far and away the island's premier industry.

The EU team were a Director, a Quality Manager (widely known affectionately as "The Banana Doctor"), the Production Advisor, and the Accounts Advisor. After two days desk-free, PC-free familiarisation in Kingstown I was invited in to meet the top management, and pushed my luck a bit by insisting on giving a presentation, a presentation of directions they might, in my view, take on the extension and computing side. The SVBGA guys perked up and showed great interest, and invited me into the bar outside for a sandwich and beer. This ran on into the afternoon, and at the MD's suggestion, we set up a series of meetings to go over their needs. These meetings I set up in the EU offices although I sensed from the EU Director that this wasn't the "done thing". He wanted to maintain a formal detachment between "his" organisation and the SVBGA management. Whatever the social connotations, it went down well with SVBGA. Gerry Schroder, the Accounts Advisor showed up at the second meeting – he'd fallen over a "cliff edge" while playing tennis (he's now a professional tennis coach in California).

He chipped in to the discussions: "I don't know what you guys make of all this stuff about action lists, seems a tad complicated. But let me tell you, when I was with CDC (Commonwealth Development Corporation) in Malawi we scoured the country for accounting software. Our needs seemed simple, to hold for each farmer various rates of interest and repayment, depending on variables like his plot size, the crop chosen and so on. So that for example we could encourage loans for some crops, and discourage loans for other crops which, like cassava (manioc, tapioca, or as we knew it fish eyes and glue!). But all the standard packages were too rigid. Then we came across SCAMPA at the Smallholder Tea Development Authority, and that fixed the problem." This tribute was naturally a delight to me.[44]

There followed for me a fascinating series of visits with the EU professionals and their counterparts covering all SVBGA's activities from farm to UK supermarket. Unexpectedly, the Vincentians fight for the top quality, end of the world banana market, as did the Chagga peasants round Kilimanjaro for Arabica coffee, who inspired us. "Small is beautiful" and can also be successful. And they use the highest of high-tech techniques – tissue cultivation (the use of tissue culture to produce identical high-yield, disease-resistant planting material) and vegetative propagation, trickle-fed fertigation (irrigation with fertiliser included), sleeved bunches (diothene plastic covers on the bunches to insect- and fungus-proof each bunch as it grows. The sleeve is peeled back briefly to de-flower the bunch at a set stage

---

[44] Was there a strong undercurrent of resentment about the EU's status among them? There often is, eg in Bangladesh, where DFID was pouring money in, but the indigenous hierarchy placed ludicrous obstacles in the way of purchasing for example. The Brit concerned was fed to the back teeth with all this. As he left the country the customs demanded that he paid full import duty on his costly personal radio. It was too much for him. He held the radio up in the air and then smashed it down on the ground into smithereens, with appropriate confrontational dialogue. It took two weeks and much consular access to get him out of the country!

announced by radio, then replaced), and finally ribbon-colour-based harvesting. The banana stogs, "trees" though they're actually plants, are identified by selected coloured ribbons when they come to flower, and the ribbon colour is used to determine the timescales which follow up to harvest. It's a fascinating process. The "hands" (about five fruits) of bananas are picked, packed, branded, and labelled in the peasant's packing shed just as you see them on the supermarket shelf.

Graphic from photo by author.

The week's colour for a particular week is announced by SVBGA over the radio, and that coloured trees' fruits are collected from the mountains to the valley collection points and then trucked down to the port. There sample hands' quality is assessed against 14 computer-held criteria on the quay in Kingstown. Failing bunches are rejected and sold for next to nothing in the town. This assessment happens again in Southampton or Portsmouth in the UK, in Holland and in

Ireland, the fruit travelling there in gas-filled holds in Geest's 6 refrigerated ships. Under the modern doctrine of "traceability",[45] integration was the SVBGA approach, right up to the degree that a defective hand of bananas could be traced back from a UK supermarket shelves to the individual grower so that problems can be resolved immediately and in very specific terms, covering the uniformity of shape, texture, and colour (but not the taste!) demanded by the supermarkets. Each bunch could be traced back immediately to its farm, which could, if need be, be warned or even decertified. This is a "Big Brother" approach which leaves you uneasy. But it's necessary for the island's economic survival. Some farmers on the steeper hillsides were losing their accreditations as competition mounted and where high-tech irrigation was not feasible because the hillside was too steep. The alternative for the Vincentians is to illegally grow cannabis up in secret clearings in the forests. The trend is for the oldies and the families to stick with bananas and traditions, while the youngsters work on drugs up in the crags.

This introduces a key strand of the EU's stance. It only became apparent to me late on. In my morning pre-breakfast snorkelling I once or twice saw through the crystal-clear water a Danforth anchor lying on the sand thirty or so feet below me. Once it had a small packet up a line floating just six feet from the surface. I snorkelled on, mildly curious, but thinking of the day's work to come.

Then, in my last week, I was joined by another British consultant, an Indian by extraction, worried about racism and

---

[45] Traceability followed the concepts first proposed in my 1969 paper to the British Computer Society, the idea that produce should be accompanied and identified by documents which enabled each item (coffee in the '69 case, hands of bananas in the case of the West Indies) to be traced back to the farmer concerned, so that quality assurance, payment etc could be assessed and rectified.

the "Tebbit Test"[46] because he was about to retire and settle in near Cambridge in the UK. I hope I reassured him. He recounted how the US drug surveillance planes monitored the movement of small fishing craft from South America in the ocean to the south of the islands. Typically the fishing craft would by sunset be moving north towards the islands. Then the night passed. And at sunrise lo and behold the same craft would be seen forging through the waves going back southwards. What had they been up to overnight? Might this spot in Umbrella Bay, I wondered, be an intermediate drugs drop off? Strengthening my impression, I went to the bar for a drink. Trying to get out again, I found I was locked in the bar and ferry transfer "cage" – like a railway station, a dark oppressive steel-gated enclave on the shore – and had to shout to get out. As I left, the bar staff had stared at me threateningly.

"Sorry about that," the manager said curtly, but with little evidence of penance and much of menace.

"Must of slammed to." But a massive steel barrier doesn't easily slam to.

Even more sinisterly, as I scrambled one dusk along a low, broken narrow wall just above the beach, round the deeply curved bay hung over with great jungle trees over the water, there was a thudding of steady footsteps behind me.

---

[46] The "Tebbit test" was suggested in 1990 by the right-wing tory MP, minister and ex-airline pilot, Norman Tebbit in a widely debated interview with the *Los Angeles Times*. He said that African and Asian immigrants should demonstrate their allegiance to the UK, as new Brits, by supporting England and Wales in any cricket matches against their old "home" country.

Graphic of landing stage by author.

"You Mr Tottle?" a deep, slow, and threatening voice demanded.

"Yes."

"You Mr Tottle from Umbrella Beach Hotel?"

"Yes."

"I don't got nothing against you. Not personally, I don't. But you should know this is a dangerous place for you to walk. A very dangerous place. Not a good place at all."

He was a big man. A very big man. The size of Viv Richards. I turned off and up to the nearest hotel and a nervous beer, then set the incident back in my mind, too absorbed in my own concerns. Only after the end of the assignment did the realities sink in. Then I went for a day's scuba diving at nearby Bequi Island. And as I followed the dive leader through a forest of swaying kelp – it wasn't good diving terrain, claustrophobic, tendrils of kelp reaching out at you – the skin of my back suddenly crawled. I felt an overpowering instinct to get away, maybe from murderers following us through the weed. The amygdala section of my brain in action perhaps, as in Lusaka previously. I gestured to the dive leader to go up to the boat. Somewhat annoyed, he refused at first, then did so.

I recalled then that all the other consultants had been told very firmly that Umbrella Beach Hotel was full. But it wasn't. Far from it. But someone didn't want inquisitive morning-snorkelling consultants around. Tourists, OK. Test teams, OK (England were then touring and everything stopped in the island to watch it). But curious consultants, no.

Should I have reported all this? Perhaps so, but who knows what threads might get drawn from it, and leading to whom? I let it lie.

However, the tale underlines some of the justification for the EU project, to encourage the banana industry and discourage the crag-based youngsters' drug-farming alternative.

Back to the SVBGA project. I toured the island first with the Production Advisor to see the activities at small-holding level and to meet the local extensionists, and to visit the research and planting material areas. Then spent a lot of time with the computing team. They were running a big and impressive organisation, with ten terminals in the main offices and others down on the quays where the data on the bananas as they came in from the fields were entered. This was followed by the results of inspections and QA, and then loading details as the fruits were packaged then crated up and loaded into the gas-filled holds of the Geest ships. Key data were extracted of course, so that the farmers' accounts could be updated, extension reports be generated and so on.

The system was developed (programmed) in ORACLE, then the leading database software worldwide, running under Netware on networked PCs. A good example of cross-Commonwealth innovation and collaboration.

My assignment was to design into this IT system the SCAMPA Extension System, so that the smallholders and extensionists could use the facilities for planning, action, and management which we have discussed earlier in the book. It took me a couple of weeks to go over and document my proposals, and to bounce them off the heads of the key departments. Then we held a key "Resolution Meeting". About twenty of the SVBGA staff were around the table, then a consultant from Trinidad, Errol Carmino, whose firm would be responsible for implementation – programming and quality assurance. The meeting took on SCAMPA concepts with enthusiasm, and Errol, one of his programmers and I spent two days in the fascinating task, using ORACLE DESIGNER, of mapping the system's data structures and functions onto the SVBGA system. You used a mouse on a screen and just dragged a target data item, e.g. plot size, from the SCAMPA source to the SVBGA equivalent. Then in processing, every occurrence of a farm's plot size would automatically cause that item in the SVBGA system to be updated. Just like that! We finished up with some extraordinarily spaghetti-like diagrams!

At this stage I bowed out, no longer my pigeon, handing over to the West Indies. It was a dramatic illustration of the advances in programming since our early days using mainframe COBOL.

I finished up by giving much of a two-day seminar to programmers and management in the HQ, St Lucia, on agricultural extension. What were the requirements and possible solutions for smallholders and for extensionists? The discussions were long and absorbing. It seemed a pleasing and fitting end to the SCAPA project, returning finally to the Windward Islands which were so closely involved in its inception. I remembered our first meetings twenty years earlier (Gordon Black, Colin Leakey, and me), with Peter Stutley and George Gwyer at DIFID about all these issues and their Winban research projects which had pursued the ideas. The West Indian banana project was a fine answer to the detractors of Empire and Commonwealth. Protecting smallholders up in the crags from competition from the mechanised capitalist monoliths of the South American mainland. What could be more worthwhile?

About the Author

After reading history at Cambridge Graham spent five years in the Uganda Protectorate Civil Service, in the South Western hills and mountains. The scenery, which is incomparable, and the people and their languages (two of which he spoke), history, and culture are drawn in depth. So are the characters, and the clash between the traditional colonial service administrators and the up-and-coming nationalists.

Then twenty years in the R&D Divisions of International Computers, starting in the earliest days, designing and programming when even operating systems had not been thought of. This gave him an abiding interest in IT, and in the key issues involved for the future of human freedom as against governmental effectiveness and law and order. This dovetails with our current debate about the "Surveillance

Society". This will, he hopes, strike sparks with the nerd community.

Then fifteen years with UN and World Bank on agricultural computing projects. This was a foray from the fields of state-of-the-art research and into what was sometimes pure, and often alarming, adventure, in twenty countries. He uses this to describe scenes in "pariah" countries like Sudan (the war zone), and from Uganda in the bad times. In Iraq he was chief consultant to Saddam Hussein's Planning Ministry when the Kuwait War broke out. He tried three times to escape, refused to work for Saddam, and went into hiding. Eventually he was rescued by Kofi Annan (Later UN Secretary General).

Graham is an MA from Cambridge and Fellow of the British Computer Society. He is author of *Point of Divergence*, a near-future novel set in Wales, the US, Manchester UK, Iraq and Uganda.

Index

Bilharzia, 80
Commonwealth, 3, 4, 7, 10, 11, 13, 21, 22, 23, 31, 54, 57, 61, 67, 82, 84, 90, 91, 92, 101, 102, 104, 105, 106, 124, 129, 130, 132, 133, 134, 135, 136, 150, 161, 162, 163, 168, 170, 172, 174, 175, 176, 177, 178, 179, 182, 187, 189
Countries
  Malaysia, 9, 16, 84, 91, 92, 95, 96, 97, 99, 101, 174
  Protectorate, 4, 31, 33, 34, 66, 68, 69, 74, 104, 108, 123, 173, 190
  Uganda, 3, 4, 7, 12, 14, 15, 16, 21, 23, 27, 29, 31, 33, 36, 38, 40, 42, 44, 45, 54, 64, 68, 69, 72, 74, 75, 77, 80, 81, 86, 87, 90, 96, 101, 102, 104, 107, 108, 109, 110, 112, 125, 126, 132, 163, 166, 167, 174, 175, 176
Crops
  Banana, 23, 104, 175, 177, 178, 179, 181, 182, 183, 187, 189
  Coffee, 46, 47, 75, 101, 123, 145, 155, 167, 182
  Cotton, 123, 177
  Vanilla, 90, 124
  Rubber, 16, 22, 84, 88, 91, 92, 95, 96, 97, 98, 99
Devonshire, 6, 21, 23, 48, 53, 106, 131
Election, 29, 30, 35, 44, 82
Empire, 4, 9, 10, 33, 39, 44, 57, 60, 70, 82, 83, 101, 104, 106, 107, 108, 109, 127, 132, 134, 136, 163, 164, 172, 175, 177, 178, 179, 189
Entomology, 7, 22, 73, 74, 75, 82
Environment, 11, 12, 21, 31, 89, 109, 125, 152, 155, 177
Extension, 16, 44, 45, 92, 94, 97, 112, 181, 187, 188
Famine, 45, 93
Groups
  ARC, 11, 91, 93
  FAO, 11, 93, 94, 95, 103, 137, 143, 144, 145, 146, 175
  RISDA, 95, 97, 98, 99, 155
  Sika, 54, 55, 57
  Sika Qualcrete, 54
Groups
  ICL, 3, 117, 118, 119, 155, 167, 168, 180
Health, 45, 64, 66, 73, 75, 92, 112
Language, 34, 47, 48, 97, 118, 130, 132, 133
LeakeyPeople
  Leakey, 116, 117, 119, 120, 122, 123, 188
Medicine, 7, 49, 64, 81
Mining, 172, 174
Molson Commission, 33, 35, 108
Muhavaura, 27
Onchocerciasis, 74, 77
People
  Baskar, 55, 56
  District Officer, 3, 11, 16, 23
  Ellis, 44, 47
  Ferguson, 4, 23, 103, 104, 109, 110
  Gwyer, 188
  Kabarega, 33, 35

Kapuscinski, 3, 5, 6, 12, 22
McCrae, 11, 73, 82, 83
Oliver, 7, 106, 152, 154, 159
Paxman, 3, 9, 10, 12, 22, 82, 104, 122, 178
Purseglove, 15, 16, 84, 86, 87
Schama, 3, 9, 22, 109
Sergeant, 4, 8
Stutley, 117, 118, 119, 120, 121, 122, 188
Tony Benn, 3, 39, 40, 44, 67, 68, 108
People
Gordon Black, 123, 188
Sharps, 44, 64, 65, 66, 71
Places
Bufumbira, 16, 26, 27, 49, 110, 112, 125, 126
Buganda, 15, 33, 34, 36, 40, 41, 68, 107
Hoima, 35, 45, 66, 112
India, 8, 13, 19, 21, 37, 54, 55, 56, 58, 91, 93, 101, 106, 112, 113
Iraq, 54, 136, 137, 138, 139, 140, 141, 144, 147, 148, 149, 150, 191
Kabale, 14, 24, 53, 54, 64, 125, 130
Kigezi, 7, 12, 15, 23, 26, 27, 28, 34, 35, 44, 48, 51, 60, 65, 66, 70, 73, 76, 82, 130, 131, 172, 174
Kolkatta, 58
Malling, 51, 52, 84, 86, 87, 88, 90, 91
Oxford, 6, 21, 23, 35, 44, 48, 49, 51, 71, 78, 79, 119, 130
Rwanda, 14, 15, 16, 27, 65, 109, 110, 112, 114, 125, 126
Sudan, 10, 22, 49, 52, 69, 81, 94, 104, 108, 136, 150, 151, 152, 155, 175, 176, 177, 191
Religion, 60, 64, 74
SCAMPA, 170, 182, 188
Scramble, 7, 69, 107, 109, 112, 160
Sport, 56, 130
Tasks
Computing, 3, 22, 55, 57, 61, 119, 121, 137, 167, 168, 170, 181, 187, 191
Industry, 16, 36, 39, 54, 57, 69, 90, 91, 96, 117, 120, 166, 167, 170, 177, 178, 181, 187
Management, 56, 94, 100, 102, 115, 152, 154, 155, 167, 181, 188
Research, 11, 15, 16, 22, 48, 57, 61, 74, 81, 84, 85, 87, 90, 91, 93, 94, 117, 119, 123, 127, 134, 139, 144, 167, 173, 187, 188, 191
Transport, 95, 108, 152, 161, 163, 166
Wildlife, 125, 127, 149

Printed in Great Britain
by Amazon